The Romantic Poets and their Circle

Richard Holmes

Published in Great Britain by National Portrait Gallery Publications,
National Portrait Gallery, St Martin's Place, London WC2H 0HE

For a complete catalogue of current publications please write to the
address above, or visit our website at www.npg.org.uk/publications

First published 1997
Second edition published 2005
This edition published 2013
Copyright © National Portrait Gallery, 1997, 2005, 2013
Text copyright © Richard Holmes, 1997, 2005, 2013

ISBN 978 1 85514 477 4

A catalogue record for this book is available from the British Library.

Managing Editor: Christopher Tinker
Editor: Andrew Roff
Design: Smith & Gilmour
Production: Geoff Barlow, Ruth Müller-Wirth
Printed and bound in China

The publisher would like to thank the copyright holders for granting
permission to reproduce works illustrated in this book. Every effort
has been made to contact the holders of copyright material, and
any omissions will be corrected in future editions if the publisher
is notified in writing.

Sold to support the National Portrait Gallery, London

Contents

Introduction – Who *were* the Romantic Poets?

The two most popular and widely read poems of the Romantic period (1770–1830) would now surprise us. They were both traditional eighteenth-century pastorals, today almost totally forgotten. The first was James Thomson's *The Seasons*, originally published in 1730 and universally admired and reprinted for over a century. ('That is true fame,' murmured Coleridge, when he found a well-worn copy thrown down in the parlour of a Devonshire inn in 1798.) The second was Robert Bloomfield's *The Farmer's Boy*, a rural idyll in rhyming couplets which sold over 60,000 copies between 1800 and 1810. Yet neither the much-loved Thomson nor the best-selling 'ploughboy poet' Bloomfield (actually a London cobbler) is a name we now associate with Romanticism.

What extraordinary force suddenly buried their reputations and brought about such a seismic shift in popular taste? One answer is simply: the dazzling Lord Byron and the intoxicating idea of the poet as 'Romantic genius'. Byron's portraits give us an unforgettable insight into this explosive notion, which still shapes (or distorts) our concept of inspiration and the creative artist. From now on the Romantic poet was young, solitary, brooding, beautiful and damned.

Byron's incarnation of this image – the dark curly locks, the mocking aristocratic eyes, the voluptuous almost feminine

Lord Byron
Richard Westall, 1813
'I am like the tyger (in poesy) if I miss my first spring – I go growling back to my jungle.'
(Letter, to his publisher John Murray, 1820)

mouth, the chin with its famous dimple and the implicit radiation of sexual danger – became famous throughout Britain after the publication of *Childe Harold's Pilgrimage* (1812). By the time of his death in Greece twelve years later, it had launched an international style. The dark clothes, the white open-necked shirt exposing the masculine throat, the aggressive display of disarray and devilry, these were the visual symbols of one archetype of Romantic genius: the Fallen Angel in rebellion. Other versions would – sooner or later – form around his contemporaries, Coleridge,

....

The Meeting of Byron and Scott at 50 Albemarle Street, Spring 1815,
an imaginary reconstruction of the scene
L. Werner, c.1850
The 'geniuses' gather in John Murray's drawing room, with Sir Walter Scott and Lord Byron in discussion at the window. The portrait over the fireplace is supposed to be that of Byron by Thomas Phillips (the cloak portrait) painted in 1813.

Keats and Shelley. Indeed Coleridge was described by his friend Lamb in 1816 as 'an Archangel a little Damaged'.

Yet if Byron was naturally the *beau ideal* of the Romantic poet, his image was deliberately manufactured and even commercially marketed. He was the most frequently painted poet of his generation: the National Portrait Gallery archives record over forty portraits and miniatures done during his lifetime, as well as several busts, medallions and even 'a wax model from life made by Madame Tussaud in 1816 before his departure for Italy'.

He was also the most self-conscious of subjects. He banned pens or books from his portraits, as being too like 'trade' and not spontaneous enough. His private letters show Byron to have been as anxious about his appearance – his weight, his hair-loss, his club foot, his careful-casual linen – as any modern film star. He was still sending for special tooth powders in the weeks immediately before his death at Missolonghi.

Thomas Phillips's famous portrait of Byron in Albanian soldier's dress (see page 93), complete with turban, jewel and dagger, was a deliberate piece of theatrical staging. Sir David Piper has described it well as 'almost Errol Flynn playing Byron', but it can also be seen as a shrewd commercial publicity shot for the author of *The Giaour*, *Lara* and *The Corsair*. Byron had bought the costume on his travels in Epirus (1809) and commissioned the portrait back in London (1813), paying for it out of his royalties.

The publisher John Murray had a copy made for his 'Poet's Gallery' in Albemarle Street, London, where it was eventually joined by trophy pictures of his other Romantic bards. Murray also skilfully controlled the engraved frontispieces to Byron's best-selling poems (*The Corsair* sold more than 10,000 copies

in its first week and 25,000 by the end of 1815). Some of these images were immediately 'improved', to conform to the popular expectations of the Romantic genius. In the engraved version of the 1813 portrait, Byron's eyes were raised apocalyptically to heaven, his hair quiffed and tinted, his brow blanched, his throat swollen with passion and even his decorative collar-pin altered from a gentleman's cameo to a large, glassy lover's keepsake.

This powerful idea of individual genius appears early in the history of Romanticism, and with a strong political impulse,

The plumb-pudding in danger: – or – state epicures taking un petit souper
(William Pitt; Napoleon Bonaparte)
James Gillray, 1805
During the Regency period, the depth of feeling against the royal and the political establishment is astonishing. In his cartoons, Gillray produced some of the most biting social satire that Britain has ever known. The protest and mockery are stinging in the satiric poems of Byron and Shelley. But the Napoleonic Wars also revived the idea of patriotism.

inspired by both the American and the French revolutions. In the striking pair of portraits by Peter Vandyke of Coleridge and Southey, commissioned by the young Bristol publisher Joseph Cottle in 1795, the two poets are shown as fiery prophets of a new age (see pages 58 and 62). They are wild, they are provocative, they are androgynous and above all they are *young*. It is no coincidence that they look extraordinarily like the student radicals of the 1960s; or rather that the student radicals – '*Imagination au pouvoir!*' – looked like them. For this was the time of the great dream of Pantisocracy, when Coleridge and Southey planned to abandon their studies and emigrate to the banks of the Susquehanna River in upper-state Pennsylvania to start European civilisation anew in an ideal American community of equal, self-governing men and women.

The poets were giving public lectures on political and moral revolution, and their portraits vividly convey the electricity of their youthful presence to an audience, with their huge eyes and wildly exaggerated hair. This 'vatic static' was much remarked on at the time by local newspaper reports in Bristol. They express a new kind of dangerous, democratic energy and romantic fervour.

When Dorothy Wordsworth first glimpsed Coleridge two years later (characteristically, he jumped over a gate and sprinted across a field to meet her) she quoted Shakespeare's definition of the inspired poet: 'He is a wonderful man. His conversation teems with soul, mind and spirit ... His eye is large and full, not dark but grey ... it speaks every emotion of his animated mind; it has more of the "poet's eye in a fine frenzy rolling" than I ever witnessed' (*Letters*, 1797). Remembering Coleridge at the same period, Hazlitt described him as swept off his feet by 'the gusts of genius'.

The circle that formed round Coleridge and Dorothy's brother William Wordsworth over the next decade revolutionised

English poetry and reanimated English prose through the highly personalised essays of Charles Lamb, William Hazlitt and Thomas De Quincey. It also began a radical change in the eighteenth-century idea of creativity and originality. The Romantic writer was revealed as essentially an inspired autobiographer, drawing on a unique inner world of experience, frequently going right back into childhood.

Hazlitt, himself trained as a painter and aesthetic philosopher, identified this emergent ideology of genius in his essays. He observed that 'Originality is necessary to genius', and described Wordsworth's genius as 'a pure emanation of the Spirit

Dove Cottage
Dove Cottage was the home of William Wordsworth from December 1799 to May 1808.
Some 80,000 people visit the cottage every year, but it remains much as it was when Wordsworth
was living there with his sister Dorothy and wife Mary, when Coleridge was a frequent visitor,
and also when Thomas De Quincey moved in as a successor to Wordsworth.

of the Age'. Keats, also writing of Wordsworth, christened this increasingly epic vision of the self as the 'egotistical Sublime' (Letter, 1818). Thus the portrait became a natural extension of the unique autobiographical self of Romanticism: a visual record of inward energies and originating power.

Yet the 'self' of the Romantic poets was by no means solitary in historical terms. A glance at their individual biographies shows how frequently their paths crossed and how often creative groups formed, as well as how rapidly they dissolved. In this sense there was not one but a whole series of Romantic circles, forever moving outwards. A geographical map of Romanticism would locate a least a dozen sacred gathering places in Britain and in Europe: the Quantock Hills in the 1790s, Grasmere in the 1800s, Lake Geneva in 1816 and Italy after 1818.

In London, such gatherings formed early round the publisher Joseph Johnson at St Paul's Churchyard (a group including Blake, Godwin, Coleridge and Mary Wollstonecraft) and later around the Lambs off Fleet Street, Leigh Hunt in Hampstead and Haydon in his chaotic City studios, each with their inimitable style of hospitality. In 1823 the painter John Doyle celebrated an entirely imaginary banquet of geniuses in *Samuel Rogers at his Breakfast Table*. In literary terms too, the Romantics were recognised as a group surprisingly soon. In 1826, two years after the death of Lord Byron in Greece, the Parisian publisher Galignani launched a new ten-volume series of contemporary British poets. With their neat octavo covers and lightweight bindings ('Cheapness and Portability'), Galignani's series was designed for the young literary 'Traveller and Economist' abroad. It was cool, smart and unstuffy: a sort of *Lonely Planet* guide to the new territory of Romanticism.

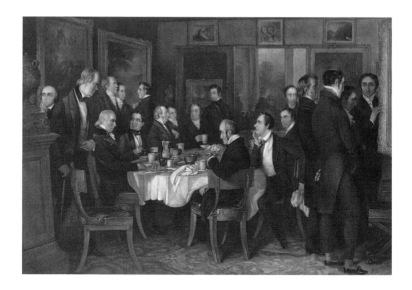

All the volumes had a portrait, a life of the author, a critical essay and a specimen of the author's handwriting 'engraved in facsimile intended to emphasise the individual romantic genius of the author' (St Clair, *The Reading Nation*). The series represented the latest in critical taste and youthful fashion, and was the first retrospective attempt to define the Romantic Circle as a group.

Galignani's selection is fascinating. Having already published Burns, his first volumes covered Byron, Scott, Wordsworth and Southey. The historic Volume 9 (1829) grouped together Coleridge, Shelley and Keats. The last volume, 10, though almost an after-thought (1839), shrewdly chose the only woman poet admitted to the series, Felicia Hemans. So a foreign publisher, neatly circumventing copyright laws, established what would remain the canonic poets of British Romanticism until the twentieth century.

There are two notable absentees: William Blake and John Clare. There are also two inclusions that might strike us as odd

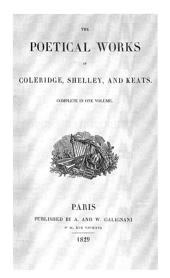

THE

POETICAL WORKS

OF

COLERIDGE, SHELLEY, AND KEATS.

COMPLETE IN ONE VOLUME.

PARIS

PUBLISHED BY A. AND W. GALIGNANI

Nº 18, RUE VIVIENNE

1829

....
LEFT

Title page of *The Poetical Works of Coleridge, Shelley and Keats*
Published by Galignani, 1829 edition

....
OPPOSITE

Samuel Rogers at his Breakfast Table, 1815
Charles Mottram, after John Doyle, c.1823
Samuel Rogers (1763–1855), banker, poet,
wit and celebrated host, regularly held breakfast
parties in St James's Place which assembled
men from many walks of life, here including
Scott (second left), Wordsworth, Southey,
Coleridge (all sitting), Byron (centre, with
head on hand) and Turner (second from right).

but are sure indicators of the shift in modern taste. Volume 2
was given up to the songs and lyrics of Tom Moore, Irish author
of the best-selling *Lalla Rookh* (1817) but now largely remembered
as Byron's witty friend and canny biographer; while Volume 6
presents George Crabbe, author of the haunting verse-tale 'Peter
Grimes' (1810) and Jane Austen's favourite poet, but now mainly
identified with Benjamin Britten's opera. Both these poets may
be due for revival. Finally, Volumes 7 and 8 are sobering reminders
of the fickleness of literary fame: group anthologies, they heap
together so many forgotten names – Rogers, Campbell,
Montgomery, White, Milman, Wilson, Cornwall ...

It is significant that Galignani's series was aimed at 'travellers'.
For the Romantic poets, in their own restless journeyings, had
almost invented certain landscapes. These quickly became the
new version of the nineteenth-century Grand Tour, and it is
astonishing how faithfully they remain the holiday destinations

of many tourists to this day. So the genius of Romanticism was also a 'spirit of place', to be found in the English Lake District, the West Country, the Highlands of Scotland, the banks of the Rhine, the Swiss lakes and Alps, the bays of Italy and the islands of Greece. You could say the Romantics had dreamed up the National Parks at home and the Club Méditerranée abroad. It was what Shelley would have called 'a pure anticipated cognition'.

The greatest painter of the age, J.M.W. Turner, progressively visited all these desirable locations (except for Greece), living rough, keeping a journal with his sketchbooks and working as a humble *plein air* artist. He first recorded them as precise topography, but eventually transformed them into places of pure vision and symbolic atmosphere. Engravings from his work later provided many of the illustrations to the poets' Collected Works as they were consolidated in the 1830s. A narrative landscape like *Snow Storm: Hannibal and his Army Crossing the Alps*, displayed at the Royal Academy in 1812, makes a clear historical reference to the Napoleonic campaigns. But it also invokes the whole idea of the Romantic traveller struggling on towards some infinitely distant destination. The Romantic self is dwarfed by the sublime terrors and energies of Nature, but also baptised by them, like Wordsworth in *The Prelude*, Coleridge in 'The Ancient Mariner' or Shelley in his ode 'To the West Wind'.

A modern extension of Romantic travel has been to make the Romantics' own houses (or at least their temporary lodgings upon earth) the sites of literary pilgrimage. This is a peculiarly British phenomenon, combining the notion of museum heritage with that of modern hagiography. Here are places of meditation and remembrance. They have become secular shrines, many administered in a priest-like way by private foundations or the

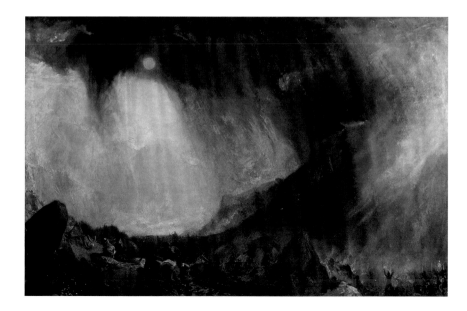

Keats House
Set in the suburb of Hampstead, London, John Keats lived in this house from 1818 to 1820 and it was where he wrote 'Ode to a Nightingale', and fell in love with Fanny Brawne, the girl next door. It is now a museum.

National Trust. They include, most famously, Wordsworth's Dove Cottage in Grasmere, Coleridge's cottage in Nether Stowey and the Keats House in Hampstead. Further afield can be found the Keats–Shelley Museum in Rome, Shelley's Casa Magni near Lerici, Tuscany, and Byron's Palazzo Mocenigo in Venice. More recherché locations might include Clare's lunatic asylum in Northampton, Mary Tighe's tomb in Ireland and Trelawny's cave on Mount Parnassus.

At home, the Britain of the Romantics presents the kind of social paradox with which we are still familiar. It was, said Coleridge, 'an Age in which Extremes Meet'. Here was a world which somehow produced both Jane Austen and John Clare, both J.M.W. Turner and James Gillray. Here was an immensely elegant society, which was also singularly drunken and dissolute. Here was a cool and self-confident society, which was also turbulent, violent and highly unstable just beneath the surface. Here was the most civilised society in Europe (the proponent of the waltz, the flushing water-closet and the seaside watercolour), which also widely condoned the pistol duel, the bare-knuckle prize fight and the teenage prostitute in the park (probably Regent's Park).

It was also what Coleridge called 'emphatically, the Age of Personality' (The Friend, 1818). It was an age of personal display, of style, of singularity. Portraiture began to flourish during the Regency, the last generation before the daguerreotype photograph. There was a growing hunger for glamorous, humourous or erotic images. Boxers, balloonists, opera singers, dragoons and actresses reappeared as tinted pin-ups for the gentleman's folding wash-screen. It was not surprising that successful writers had their profiles engraved as frontispieces to their works. National figures achieved the apotheosis of being elevated to huge wooden pub signs, or received the fatal accolade of a cartoon by Gillray, Cruikshank or Rowlandson. Thanks to new print technology, these were reproduced by the thousand. Ironically, such notoriety, then as now, was prized even by its victims. The Prince of Wales paid vast sums to collect the originals of Gillray's cartoons of himself.

The Romantic idea of genius produced a celebrity culture of heroes and villains (often rapidly interchangeable) which is also startlingly familiar to us. The patriotic fame of Nelson was a new phenomenon and was characteristically celebrated by a fine, all-action biography by the poet Southey (1813); but he and Emma Hamilton were also pilloried by Gillray. Cult love-hate figures like Pitt and Napoleon dominated the political stage and appeared ceaselessly in the poetry, journalism, painting and caricatures of the day. In 1822 a national subscription (ladies-only) paid for the erection of a naked statue of Achilles in honour of the Duke of Wellington at Hyde Park Corner. It's still there, like Nelson's Column in Trafalgar Square (1842); and there are still more 'Wellington' and 'Nelson' pub signs than any other in England.

TOP

Illustration from Pierce Egan's
Life in London
George Cruikshank, 1821

BOTTOM

Dido, in despair! (Emma Hamilton)
James Gillray, 1801

A buxom Lady Hamilton dissolves into tears
as Nelson sails away, and Sir William sleeps.
The title refers to the desertion of Dido,
Queen of Carthage, by her lover, Aeneas.

Horatio Nelson, Viscount Nelson
Lemuel Francis Abbott, 1797

....
LEFT
James Belcher
Unknown artist, c.1800

....
OPPOSITE
**Theatrical mendicants, relieved
(Sarah Siddons; Charles Kemble;
John Philip Kemble; Hugh Percy,
2nd Duke of Northumberland)**
James Gillray, 1809

Similarly in the sporting world, fencers, jockeys, swimmers and long-distance runners began to gain national recognition (and often nicknames). Bare-knuckle boxers like Tom Cribb and Jem Belcher attracted huge personal followings (and wagers), and gained a new kind of glamour. Hazlitt attended a prize fight near Newbury in 1821 in which Bill Neate fought Tom 'The Gasman' Hickman for a combined purse of £200,000. The young, handsome and gentlemanly Belcher was idolised by Hazlitt and Byron, and had a lively fan club among the senior members of the Royal Academy. Renowned for his courage, his cravats and (like Nelson) his lost eye, Belcher has been described as 'a Romantic poet among pugilists'. He died at the age of thirty-two.

The influence of Romantic genius was most apparent in the London theatre. Driven by the rivalry between the houses of Drury Lane and Covent Garden, late eighteenth-century productions had been dominated by the actor-manager John

Philip Kemble and his sister, the great tragic actress Sarah
Siddons. Their style was solemn, ornate and strictly classical,
and their approach businesslike and highly respectable. (Mrs
Siddons would not visit Mary Wollstonecraft after her affair with
Godwin.) But with the burning down of their Covent Garden
theatre in 1808 and the breaking of their monopoly, a new kind
of intensely charismatic and emotional actor began to appear.

With Edmund Kean and Dorothy Jordan private lives and
public theatre overlapped, often scandalously, and produced
a new expressive style of acting, and a new sense of Romantic
authenticity. This was especially true in their reinterpretations of
Shakespeare's plays, with Kean revolutionising the notion of the
tragic villain and outsider, while Jordan brought back to life the
wit and tenderness of the Shakespearean heroine. Keats's play
Otto the Great was specifically written for Kean. The Shakespeare
lectures of both Coleridge and Hazlitt drew directly on the
spontaneous psychology of these actors, and effectively

....
LEFT
Charles Waterton
Charles Wilson Peale, 1824

....
OPPOSITE
James Northcote
Self-portrait, 1784

transformed Shakespeare himself into a Romantic author. Coleridge's great essay 'Shakespeare's Judgement Equal to his Genius' (1808) became a central statement of Romantic doctrine.

What is far less well known is that the world of science also produced Romantic figures, whose discoveries were seen as great adventures of the mind. William Herschel, with his discovery of the seventh planet Uranus in 1781 and his theories of galaxies outside the Milky Way, made astronomy the most popular science of the age and a field in which theological problems of the Creation, and extraterrestrial life, could be imaginatively discussed. The chemist Humphry Davy proved one of the most brilliant public lecturers of the day, drawing huge audiences to the Royal Institution in Albemarle Street (opposite Byron's publisher Murray), as well as inventing the miners' safety lamp.

Mary Shelley partly based the ambitions of Dr Frankenstein on what she had heard in Davy's lectures on the future of chemistry and electrical power. Eccentric explorers and zoologists like Charles Waterton (1782–1865), who travelled for years alone in South America and the West Indies, also opened up the horizons of Romantic knowledge and brought a new sense of a global environment with his autobiographical *Wanderings* (1825).

Embracing all these figures, Romantic portrait painting concentrated on a new, quiet psychological penetration of character. It required the artistic rendering of inner landscapes, of interiority. This was not the world of the great flamboyant society painters of the day: Reynolds, Hoppner and Lawrence. It was the domain of small-time professionals and often of amateurs. One of the most successful practitioners was James Northcote, RA (1746–1831),

John Opie
Self-portrait, 1785

who painted plain but noble studio portraits of Godwin and Coleridge, and numerous self-portraits. Significantly he posed himself with paintbrushes in one hand and the other pointing pensively to his brow, to indicate the inward source of all artistic power. Hazlitt wrote an entire book about him, *Boswell Redivus: or, Conversations of James Northcote* (1827), constructed from a series of personal interviews, which is itself a Romantic form, seeking for autobiographical revelations and confessions (or at least good gossip).

Thomas Phillips, RA (1770–1845), also based much of his career on commissioned portraiture, producing notable studies of Blake, Byron, Coleridge and Davy. He was particularly admired for the 'noble gloom' with which he revealed the Romantic intensity of his sitters. In 1818 it was he whom John Murray commissioned to produce a whole gallery of literary portraits in Albemarle Street.

It is one of the features of the Romantic Circle that so many of their portraits were painted by personal friends, like Haydon, John Opie, Amelia Curran, William Hazlitt, Washington Allston and Joseph Severn. Opie's tender portraits of his wife Amelia and of her friend Mary Wollstonecraft are masterpieces (see pages 67 and 43). These paintings have a strong biographical element, a sense of shared intimacy and conversational directness. They have the tender feel of treasured souvenirs. At the same time, they powerfully suggest the intense solitary inner life of the sitters, an extraordinary haunting quality of self-reflection and self-awareness. This is particularly true of the many portraits and sketches of Keats, nearly all of them amateur. For the painters, the problem of rendering the inward quality of Romantic genius, the workings of the imagination as an interior force (no longer represented by external Muses), had become the new touchstone of Romantic authenticity.

The American painter Washington Allston (1779–1843), when trying to capture the fluctuating genius of his friend Coleridge in middle age (see page 61), remarked on the supreme difficulty of rendering this essential, inward, fleeting quality of the poet's mysterious power:

So far as I can judge the likeness is a true one. But it is Coleridge in repose, and though not unstirred by the perpetual groundswell of his everworking intellect ... it is not Coleridge in his highest mood – the poetic state. When in that state no face I ever saw was like his, it seemed almost spirit made visible, without a shadow of the physical upon it. But it was beyond the reach of my art. (*Life and Letters*, 1893)

The notion of Romantic genius as fleeting and ephemeral, doomed to die young or remain unrecognised by the general public (a subject of obsessive meditation by Haydon in his *Journals*), gradually modulated the pictorial style. Several painters, like Hilton, Severn and Curran, unsatisfied with their first attempts, returned to their canvases after the sitter's death. Their portraiture thus takes on a memorial quality, the immediate 'likeness' becoming subtly overlaid with retrospective feelings of tragic loss, of 'intimations of mortality' and the haunting sense of historical grandeur not fully recognised in the sitter's own lifetime. Thus some of the most famous images of Keats and Shelley are in fact true 'icons': not made from life but composed from sacred memory, an attempt to go beyond death.

Indeed the idea of early death seems inseparable from Romanticism, and it was painfully true of Keats (twenty-five), Shelley (twenty-nine), Byron (thirty-six), Mary Wollstonecraft (thirty-eight) and Burns (thirty-eight), not to mention Jem Belcher (thirty-two), where the sense of 'unfulfilled renown' is overwhelming. But bearing in mind that the average lifespan in the English Regency was not much more than fifty (an age achieved by Hazlitt, Davy and Mary Shelley), it is less often remarked how many of the Romantic group achieved a comparatively ripe old age. Wordsworth, Godwin and Herschel lived into their eighties; Turner, Hunt, De Quincey, Clare and Blake into their seventies. Nonetheless, the individual biographies reveal what a high proportion of all their lives, long or short, was disrupted or ended by poverty, insanity, drug addiction, alcoholism or suicide (actual or attempted). And as Virginia Woolf observed, 'The true length of a person's life, whatever the DNB may say, is always a matter of dispute' (*Orlando*, 1928).

Joseph Severn
Self-portrait, c.1820

The question of literary recognition, or neglect, is harder
to assess. It touches on complex issue of changing tastes and
shifting reputations. Burns, Byron, Scott and Felicia Hemans
(all identified by Galignani) achieved huge popular success
in their lifetimes and immediately afterwards. But Hemans was
forgotten after the First World War and Walter Scott is currently
unfashionable (until perhaps revived by Scottish Independence).
Within a generation Wordsworth had become a national
institution and Coleridge a national scandal, positions they
have both magnificently maintained. Shelley's reputation was
upheld by pirate publications, and the saintly (almost fatal)
dedication of his wife and the Shelley Society, until successfully
radicalised again by twentieth-century scholarship.

John Keats
Joseph Severn, 1819

By contrast, William Blake was completely forgotten outside a tiny circle by the time of his death, and his works remained out of print for a generation, until unexpectedly revived by Gilchrist's brilliant Victorian biography of 1863. The research so exhausted its author that he died before publication, leaving the biography to be finished by his wife. Similarly, Keats was not widely read until Monckton Milnes's biography of 1848, and his subsequent championing by the Pre-Raphaelite painters and editors. John Clare had to wait until the late twentieth century to be fully published and rediscovered, and placed in context by Jonathan Bate's biography of 2003. For Leigh Hunt that process is just beginning (see Select bibliography).

The position of women writers within the Romantic Circle is particularly anomalous. Jane Austen is now a cult

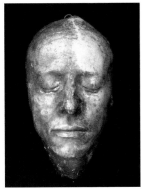
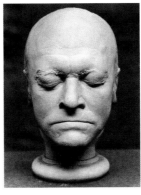
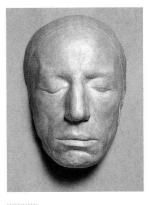

....
**John Keats, plaster
cast of death-mask**
Unknown artist, 1821

....
William Blake, life-mask
James S. Deville, 1823

....
**William Wordsworth,
plaster cast of life-mask**
Benjamin Robert Haydon, 1815

Romantic genius always ready for renewal and reawakening.

figure, but was not widely admired until Austen Leigh's *Memoir*
of 1870. By contrast, Mary Wollstonecraft was apparently doomed
to a century of obscurity by the noble, well-intentioned *Memoirs* of
her husband in 1798. Mary Robinson, one of the most glamorous
figures of her entire generation, sank into complete oblivion until
suddenly recovered by two simultaneous biographies in 2004.
Many other women poets, like Mary Tighe and Laetitia Landon,
remain unjustly forgotten – at least up to the present date
(see pages 104–5).

So what Coleridge called 'true fame' is still fickle and
uncertain. Yet the genius of the Romantic poets seems infinitely
renewable. Their wonderful circle of creative energy still
pulses out towards us, always challenging, always surprising,
always expanding. One mark of genius, said Goethe, is
posthumous productivity.

BIOGRAPHIES

....

CLOCKWISE FROM TOP LEFT

William Wordsworth
Robert Hancock, 1798

Samuel Taylor Coleridge
Robert Hancock, 1796

Robert Southey
Robert Hancock, 1796

Charles Lamb
Robert Hancock, 1798

The Unknown Romantics

In 1796 the Bristol bookseller Joseph Cottle began commissioning pencil drawings of a number of unknown young poets whose work he thought might have a future. Over the next two years he published four of them with engravings of their portraits by Robert Hancock as the frontispieces to their books.

Cottle's selection was astonishingly prescient. All four of his poets were in their twenties, without literary recognition of any kind, and with undistinguished backgrounds and very chequered early careers. Yet these curiously stiff and vulnerable little profiles, which seem almost like naïve photo-booth images, can be seen now as their passport pictures to future fame.

William Wordsworth (1770–1850) was from Cumberland and, after graduating from Cambridge, had lived for some time in revolutionary France, where he had fathered an illegitimate child by his lover Annette Vallon.

Samuel Taylor Coleridge (1772–1834) was from Devon, had left Cambridge without a degree and, under the pseudonym Silas Tomkyn Comberbache, temporarily joined the 15th Light Dragoons, from which he was discharged as 'insane'.

Robert Southey (1774–1843) was from Bristol, had graduated from Oxford and was planning to establish a utopian community in America ('Pantisocracy') and to lecture with Coleridge on revolutionary politics.

Charles Lamb (1775–1834) was born in London, had attended Christ's Hospital School with Coleridge and, after his sister Mary had gone briefly but spectacularly mad (she murdered their mother), had joined the East India Company as an office clerk.

Their early collaborative works included a verse-play, *The Fall of Robespierre* (1794, Southey and Coleridge); a selection of the early *Poems* (1797, Coleridge and Lamb); and the first great collection of the English Romantic movement, *Lyrical Ballads* (1798, Wordsworth and Coleridge). The *Lyrical Ballads* astonished the reading public with its directness of style and challenging subject matter in such poems as 'The Ancient Mariner', 'The Mad Mother', 'The Idiot Boy', 'The Thorn' and 'Tintern Abbey'. The first Romantic Circle had been formed and would be soon followed by many others.

William Blake (1757–1827)

Poet, painter and engraver, William Blake grew up in London 'conversing with angels' and retained a visionary view of the world throughout his long, hard-working and poverty-stricken career. His *Songs of Innocence and of Experience* (1794) – which contained such lyric masterpieces as 'The Sick Rose', 'The Tyger' and 'London' – sold fewer than thirty copies in his lifetime.

Powerfully influenced by the revolutions in America and France, and an idiosyncratic form of Swedenborgian mysticism, he created a series of illuminated 'prophetic books', including *Visions of the Daughters of Albion* (1793), *The Four Zoas* (1804), *Milton* (1808) and *Jerusalem* (1820). Well known in the radical circle of

William Blake
Bronze cast, 1953, of a life-mask
by James S. Deville of 1823
This bronze head was cast from
the plaster life-mask executed
by the sculptor and phrenologist
James Deville in 1823 to illustrate
the 'Faculty of Imagination'. The
cannonball skull and closed eyes
vividly suggest the power and
inwardness of Blake's visions.

William Blake
Thomas Phillips, 1807

Mary Wollstonecraft, Tom Paine and William Godwin, he retained a fierce, eccentric independence and was arrested on a charge of treason at Chichester in 1803, though found not guilty. His antinomian views are memorably expressed in 'The Proverbs of Hell' (1790) with aphoristic force: 'The tigers of wrath are wiser than the horses of instruction.'

Blake's marriage to the beautiful Catherine Boucher, daughter of a London market gardener, with whom he sunbathed naked in his garden at Lambeth, was childless but intensely happy. Towards the end of his life his poetry was recognised by Coleridge, Wordsworth and Southey, and he was extensively interviewed on his beliefs by the journalist Henry Crabb Robinson. He attracted a circle of young followers, including the painters John Linnell and Samuel Palmer, who called themselves 'The Ancients' in his honour. He died singing at Fountain Court, off the Strand. His beautiful poem from Milton, known as 'Jerusalem', has become adopted as the 'alternative' British national anthem: 'And did those feet in ancient time/ Walk upon England's mountains green?'

His disciple Frederick Tatham described Blake as short, stocky and energetic, with strange prominent blue eyes and a habit of constantly rolling a pencil, paintbrush or engraver's burin between his fingers. 'My fingers Emit sparks of fire with Expectation of my future labours,' wrote Blake. 'I have very little of Mr Blake's company,' said Catherine once, 'he is always in Paradise.'

Thomas Phillips's portrait was commissioned by the publisher R.H. Cromek and shows Blake sitting uneasily in the corner of a mahogany bench, uncharacteristically wearing a smart white waistcoat and cravat, and a gold seal on a red

ribbon, the outfit of a successful small businessman. The tense
position, upward glance and poised right hand holding a pencil
suggest Blake's mind is on higher things and he is impatient
to get back to work. Phillips later recalled that during the sitting
Blake described a vision of the Archangel Gabriel ascending
through his studio ceiling.

A disturbing hint of the gargoyle animates John Linnell's
penetrating study of Blake in old age. The drawing is based on
one of Linnell's own ivory miniatures (1821; Fitzwilliam Museum,
Cambridge) and was copied by the artist in 1861 for Gilchrist's
biography (1863). For this later version Linnell allowed himself
a freer retrospective interpretation of Blake's visionary power.

Robert Burns (1759–96)

Scottish national poet, exquisite love-song writer and incorrigible philanderer, Burns grew up on his father's poverty-stricken farm in Ayrshire and could genuinely be described as a ploughboy poet. He said his first poems were inspired at fifteen by 'a bewitching, bonnie, sweet, sonsie lass' working beside him in the fields at harvest time – 'thus with me began Love and Poesy' (autobiographical letter, August 1787). Volatile and seductive, a fine dancer and fiddle-player, Burns was also a passionate student of English, Scottish and French poetry, and soon developed a sophisticated knowledge of Highland folklore. The failure of a farming project with his long-suffering brother Gilbert, together with a chaotic series of tangled love affairs (resulting in two illegitimate children), determined Burns to 'quit his native country forever' and emigrate to Jamaica. But the unexpected literary success of his *Poems, Chiefly in the Scottish Dialect* (1786) led to fame and lionisation in Edinburgh. His early pieces included the bawdy 'Cotter's Saturday Night', the caustic 'Holy Willie's Prayer' and the infinitely touching 'To a Mouse, on Turning Her Up in Her Nest with the Plough', which begins 'Wee, sleekit, cow'rin, tim'rous beastie …'. In 1788 Burns married and attempted to settle down, obtaining work as an excise officer in Dumfriesshire, while contributing over two hundred songs to James Johnson's classic folk anthology *The Scots Musical Museum*, quixotically refusing all payment. These wonderful vernacular lyrics included 'Auld Lang Syne', 'O my Luv's like a red, red Rose', 'Scots wha hae' (a battle song), 'The Banks o' Doon', 'Highland Mary', 'John Anderson, my Jo', the heartbreaking 'Ae Fond Kiss' and the revolutionary refrain 'A Man's a man, for a' That'.

Robert Burns
Alexander Nasmyth, c.1821–2

Walter Scott described the poet's eye as remarkably large, dark and glowing – 'I say it literally glowed
… I never saw such another eye in a human head.' Byron loved Burns's 'antithetical mind – tenderness,
roughness – delicacy, coarseness – sentiment, sensuality – soaring and groveling – dirt and deity –
all mixed up in that one compound of inspired clay!' (*Journal*, 1813).

After producing nine legitimate children, Burns 'fell asleep upon the snow' (Lockhart, 1830), on his way home from a festive tavern dinner in February 1796, and died shortly thereafter from rheumatic heart disease. The celebration of Burns Night (25 January) by Scottish patriotic clubs began almost immediately in 1801, and eventually spread around the globe. Wordsworth delighted in the rumbustious tale of 'Tam O'Shanter' (1791) and soberly praised Burns as an archetypal Romantic figure: the poet 'who walked in glory and in joy/ Following his plough along the mountainside' ('Resolution and Independence', 1802). Lamb declared that in his youth 'Burns was the god of my idolatry', while Hazlitt remarked that 'he would rather have written one song of Burns's than all the epics of Walter Scott' (*Select British Poets*, 1824) – a very Irish compliment.

Mary Wollstonecraft (1759–97)

An inspiration for the British feminist movement, Mary Wollstonecraft was also the author of travel books, short stories, novels and influential works on children's education. Half-Irish by birth, tempestuous and articulate by nature, she started a school in Newington Green with her great friend Fanny Blood, travelled in Portugal and settled in London in 1787, working as a journalist and translator for the radical publisher Joseph Johnson. There she met Tom Paine, William Blake and William Godwin, and in 1792 published *A Vindication of the Rights of Woman*.

She lived in Paris during the French Revolution and had a child by the American Gilbert Imlay. In 1795 she travelled in Scandinavia, published *A Short Residence in Sweden, Norway and Denmark* and, abandoned by Imlay, tried to commit suicide by throwing herself into the River Thames. She fell in love with Godwin, conceived a second daughter – the future Mary Shelley – but died in childbirth at the age of thirty-eight. Godwin wrote her biography in 1798, which caused great scandal, and Shelley put her into his revolutionary poem *The Revolt of Islam* (1817).

Handsome and dashing, with an unruly mass of auburn hair, she was frequently painted by her contemporaries. The novelist Amelia Alderson, who had been her rival in love for William Godwin, once remarked: 'Everything I ever saw for the first time always disappointed me, except for Mary Wollstonecraft and the Cumberland Lakes.'

John Opie's portrait (c.1797) was painted in London, when Mary Wollstonecraft was pregnant with her second child, and Godwin kept the picture above the desk in his study for the rest of his life.

Mary Wollstonecraft
John Opie, c.1797

In *Memoirs* (1798), William Godwin gave his impression of Mary Wollstonecraft in love:
'Her whole character seemed to change with her change of fortune. Her sorrows, the depression
of spirits, were forgotten, and she assumed all the simplicity and vivacity of a youthful mind ... .
She was playful, full of confidence, kindness and sympathy. Her eyes assumed new lustre, and
her cheeks new colour and smoothness. Her voice became cheerful; her temper overflowing
with universal kindness; and that smile of bewitching tenderness from day to day illuminated
her countenance, which all who knew her will so well recollect.'

William Godwin (1756–1836)

With his concepts of social justice, equality and fearless self-expression, the political philosopher and popular novelist William Godwin had a profound effect on many of the Romantics in their idealistic youth, including Coleridge, Wordsworth, Hazlitt and Shelley. Born in the misty fenlands of East Anglia, Godwin was educated at Hoxton Academy, London, in preparation for the Dissenting ministry, but his wide reading in the French *philosophes* such as Voltaire and Condorcet converted him to atheistic and anarchist views tending towards revolutionary Jacobinism.

Godwin's great work *An Enquiry Concerning Political Justice* (1793) proposed republican and communitarian ideas, and attacked many institutions such as private property, marriage and the established Church, and became notorious for its defence of 'free love'. He defended a number of leading working-class radicals, including John Thelwall, in the famous Treason Trials of 1794. 'Wherever liberty, truth, justice was the theme, his name was not far off' (Hazlitt, 1825).

A shy, modest and intensely intellectual man, he was transformed by his marriage to Mary Wollstonecraft and devastated by her early death in childbirth. Their daughter, Mary, subsequently ran away with his most devoted young disciple, Shelley. In later life he was harried by debts and the organising capacities of his second wife, Mrs Clairmont. He ran a bookshop from his house in Skinner Street, Holborn, and tried to make a living from a series of thriller novels, including *Caleb Williams* (1794), *Fleetwood* (1805) and *Mandeville* (1817).

Godwin's face – 'fine, with an expression of placid temper and recondite thought' (Hazlitt) – with its high intellectual

William Godwin
James Northcote, 1802

forehead usually surmounted by a twinkling pair of round gold spectacles, entirely belied his reputation as a political firebrand. Shelley's first wife, Harriet, described Godwin after she had seen him in his study in 1812, shortly before Shelley had the fatal meeting with his daughter: 'His manners are so soft and pleasing that I defy even an enemy to be displeased with him ... . Have you ever seen a bust of Socrates, for his head is very much like that?' Even so, Godwin's name always remained associated with a Romantic idea of social progress. 'Truth is omnipotent ... Man is perfectible, or in other words susceptible of perpetual improvement' (Political Justice). In 1825 Hazlitt observed how Godwin had mellowed:

> In private, the author of Political Justice, at one time reminded those who knew him of the Metaphysician grafted on the Dissenting Minister. There was a dictatorial, captious, quibbling pettiness of manner. He lost this with the first blush and awkwardness of popularity ... . He is, at present, as easy as an old glove ... . There is a very admirable likeness of him by Mr Northcote. (The Spirit of the Age, 1825)

....
OPPOSITE

William Godwin
William Brockedon, 1832
The former political firebrand ended his days as Yeoman Usher in the House of Commons, with a state pension and all his fiction re-issued in Bentley's Standard Novels.

2 . 6 . 32

Benjamin Robert Haydon (1786 –1846)

Passionately (but wrongly) convinced of his own destiny as a great history painter, Haydon put his true genius into five volumes of anguished and exuberant *Journals* (1804–46), which recount his heroic struggles with incomparable gusto. Both intimate and operatic, they dramatise the Romantic artist's life in London: his moments of candlelit inspiration, his stormy friendships, his erotic dreams, his Napoleonic fantasies (he painted more than twenty-five versions of *Napoleon Musing at St Helena*), and his frequent imprisonments for debt.

Charismatic, self-opinionated and deeply religious, Haydon attracted to his chaotic studio rooms the inner circle of Romantic writers, including at various times Lamb, Coleridge, Scott, Hazlitt, Wordsworth, Hunt, Shelley and Keats. His wonderful accounts include Hazlitt driven mad by love, Shelley hot-gospeling atheism

and Mrs Siddons terrifying the servants with her sepulchral rendition of Lady Macbeth. In December 1817 he hosted the 'Immortal Dinner' when Wordsworth told jokes, Lamb got drunk and Keats proposed the toast: 'Newton's health, and confusion to Mathematics!' The heads of Wordsworth, Newton and Keats appear in his enormous canvas *Christ's Entry into Jerusalem*, which took six years to complete (1814–20) and a further three years to

....

OPPOSITE

Benjamin Robert Haydon

Sir David Wilkie, 1815

The chalk study of Haydon asleep in his studio apparently shows a contented man dreaming of fame. Yet, for most of his life, Haydon was tortured by his inability to fulfil his overwhelming ambition to 'paint like Titian and draw like Raphael'. 'Poor Haydon,' exclaimed Elizabeth Barrett Browning, 'Think what an agony life was to him, so constituted! – his own genius a clinging curse!'

....

ABOVE

Christ's Entry into Jerusalem

Benjamin Robert Haydon, 1814–20

Grouped in the top right hand corner are Newton (extreme right), Wordsworth (monkishly looking down) and Keats (in profile, immediately above) in animated discussion with his friend the painter William Bewick.

Benjamin Robert Haydon
Georgiana Margaretta Zornlin, 1825

sell (at a loss). Later monumental paintings include *The Raising of Lazarus* (1820–23), *The Reform Banquet* (1832–4) and *The Anti-Slavery Society Convention* (1840–41). But his masterpiece was a rapidly executed portrait, *Wordsworth on Helvellyn* (1842; see page 57), which, as Hazlitt observed brilliantly, caught the ageing poet's 'drooping weight of thought and expression'. Despite his *Lectures on Painting*, his successful pupils (including Sir Edwin Landseer) and his quixotic support of the Elgin Marbles, Haydon was never elected to the Royal Academy and eventually committed suicide in his studio, in front of an unfinished canvas. 'The solitary grandeur of Historical Painting is gone,' he wrote. 'There was something grand, something poetical, something mysterious, in pacing your quiet Painting Room after midnight, with a great work lifted up on a gigantic easel' (*Journal*, 2 October 1844).

James Gillray (1757–1815)

No form of art could be considered less Romantic and more ephemeral than the personal caricature. Yet the graphic work of Gillray, a caricaturist of relentless ferocity and seething imagination, permanently stamped the sensibility of his age. The natural heir to Hogarth, a superb draughtsman and engraver, Gillray added a unique element of satirical malevolence, directed against power, beauty or celebrity. His victims included many of the leading political, literary and aristocratic figures of the

James Gillray
Self-portrait, c.1800

Promis'd Horrors of the French INVASION, — or — Forcible Reasons for negociating a Regicide PEACE. Vide, The Authority of Edmund Burke.

day (who were often, like the Prince Regent, his most assiduous collectors); but he was especially merciless to the royal family and their scandalous excesses.

Born in London of strict Moravian parents (who forbade all games and entertainments), Gillray lived at home till the age of thirty-six and never married. Trained in the Royal Academy Schools (like Blake), but unable to support himself by conventional illustration, he suddenly found his vein producing topical caricatures for the publisher Hannah Humphrey in 1791. He was assigned rooms above her fashionable printshop at 18 Old Bond Street, and began pouring forth a weekly flood of reckless, uncensored etchings. Wraith-like French Jacobins are depicted lynching the portly English Club men of St James's in *The Promis'd horrors of the French invasion* (1796). Radical young poets such as Coleridge, Southey and Charles Lamb appear as grotesque animals in the *New morality* (1798). The scientist Humphry Davy is shown sniggering at the farts produced by *Scientific researches! – new discoveries in pneumaticks!* at the Royal Institution (1802, see page 90). Pitt and Napoleon voraciously carve up the globe with cutlasses in *The plumb-pudding in danger* (1805, see page 8). Even national heroes like Nelson do not escape Gillray's lash, especially when attached to a buxom mistress like Emma Hamilton (*Dido, in despair!*, 1801, see page 18). 'No one would guess this gaunt, bespectacled figure, this dry man, was a great artist,' wrote the German journalist Huttner. The government tried to curb him with a £200 pension, but Gillray began drinking heavily, and from 1807 his work became increasingly nightmarish. Confined to his rooms at Mrs Humphrey's, he tried to throw himself from an upper window but became stuck in the iron bars. He was officially diagnosed as insane in 1811, and when the young illustrator George Cruikshank called upon his hero, he was dismayed to be told: 'My name is not Gillray, but Rubens.'

OPPOSITE

The Promis'd horrors of the French invasion, – or – forcible reasons for negotiating a regicide peace
James Gillray, 1796
French revolutionary troops storm down St James's, while Charles James Fox flagellates the Prime Minister William Pitt, Tory members of White's Club are lynched from their balcony, and Whig members of Brooke's Club mount a pro-French guillotine.

William Wordsworth (1770–1850)

The greatest poet of his age, who can be properly compared to Shakespeare and Milton for his noble conception of mankind in nature, William Wordsworth dedicated his whole life to poetry and only came slowly into his powers. His two major poems were largely composed in his thirties and forties: his verse autobiography, The Prelude (1805, revised 1850), and his philosophic epic, The Excursion (1814). He was the son of a Cumberland attorney, born at Cockermouth and educated at Hawkshead Grammar School in the Lake District. After Cambridge, Wordsworth travelled and lived in France, where he witnessed the early stages of the Revolution.

Wordsworth settled near Coleridge at Alfoxden in the Quantock Hills and together they published Lyrical Ballads (1798). After a period in Germany, Wordsworth finally returned to Grasmere in 1799, where he remained until his death. His passionate friendship with his younger sister Dorothy, whose famous Journal (1798–1803) describes their life together at Alfoxden and Grasmere in exquisite natural detail, shaped and sustained his entire career. (Ironically, Dorothy avoided having her own portrait painted and only a paper silhouette is known; see page 56.)

The shorter lyrics published in Poems in Two Volumes (1807), including the mysterious 'Lucy' poems, 'Daffodils' and his 'Ode: On the Intimations of Immortality from Recollections of Early Childhood', slowly established his reputation among a generation of younger admirers (such as Thomas De Quincey). Happy in his marriage to Mary Hutchinson and increasingly conservative in his views, he was appointed Stamp Distributor for Westmorland in 1813, wrote a Guide to the Lakes in 1822 and was appointed Poet Laureate in 1843.

William Wordsworth
Benjamin Robert Haydon, 1818

Tall, taciturn and weatherbeaten, with a deep Cumberland voice and commanding presence, he impressed everyone he met with a sense of inner power. His appearance in 1798 was described by Hazlitt as 'gaunt and Don Quixote-like', with eccentric touches:

He was quaintly dressed (accordingly to the costume of that unconstrained period) in a brown fustian jacket and striped pantaloons. There was something of a roll, a lounge in his gait, not unlike his own Peter Bell. There was a severe, worn pressure of thought about his temples, a fire in his eye (as if he saw something in objects more than the outward appearance), an intense high narrow forehead, a Roman nose, cheeks furrowed by strong purpose and feeling, and a convulsive inclination to laughter about the mouth, a good deal at variance with the solemn, stately expression of the rest of the face. (*My First Acquaintance with Poets*, 1823)

The painter Haydon was fascinated by him and executed the chalk drawing on page 55 in 1818 as a gift for Wordsworth's wife, Mary: 'He sat like a Poet and Philosopher, calm, quiet, amiable. I succeeded in a capital likeness of him.' Wordsworth later called the drawing 'The Brigand'.

Wordsworth remained an active fell-walker into old age and climbed Helvellyn to celebrate his seventieth birthday. Haydon marked this feat with the full-length picture illustrated opposite, which was actually executed from sittings in his London studio but with the symbolic setting of Helvellyn at sunset painted in afterwards from memory. With its intense, brooding inwardness, it is one of the great successes of Romantic portraiture.

LEFT
Dorothy Wordsworth
Unknown artist, 1806

OPPOSITE
William Wordsworth
Benjamin Robert Haydon, 1842

Samuel Taylor Coleridge (1772–1834)

'Poet and philosopher-in a-mist' (according to his own description), fell-walker, lecturer and opium addict, Coleridge is the great inspirational figure of English Romanticism. Wordsworth called him 'the only wonderful man I ever knew'. Born at Ottery St Mary, Devon, the son of a clergyman, he attended Cambridge University, volunteered for the Dragoons, collaborated with Wordsworth on the *Lyrical Ballads* (1798), studied in Germany and settled for four years at Keswick in the Lake District. This period saw the writing of his most famous poems, 'Kubla Khan', 'The Ancient Mariner', 'Christabel', 'Frost at Midnight' and 'Dejection: an Ode'.

Thereafter, his marriage broken by a disastrous love affair (see the 'Asra' poems) and health wrecked by opium, he travelled restlessly in the Mediterranean, lectured on poetry in London and Bristol, and in 1816 finally settled at Highgate in the care of the surgeon James Gillman, where he wrote his *Aids to Reflection*, and many late poems such as 'Limbo' and 'Alice Du Clos'. His *Biographia Literaria* (1817), his collected essays in *The Friend* (1818) and his superb *Notebooks* (1794–1834) all give a vivid impression of his troubled genius.

Coleridge was a marvellous talker and autobiographer, as shown in his self-mocking description in a letter written shortly after the Vandyke portrait was painted for his publisher, Cottle, in 1795. This was not so much modesty as a Romantic sense of his own peculiarities, in which chaotic inner energy was bodied forth as weakness and eccentricity:

My face, unless when animated by immediate eloquence, expresses great Sloth, & great, indeed almost idiotic good-nature. 'Tis a mere carcass of a face, fat flabby and expressive chiefly of inexpression. My gait is awkward, & the walk, & the Whole man indicates indolence capable of energies ... . I have read almost everything – a library-cormorant – I am deep in all out of the way books ... . Metaphysics, & Poetry, & 'Facts of Mind' ... . I cannot breathe thro' my nose – so my mouth, with sensual thick lips, is almost always open. In conversation I am impassioned ... . (Letter to John Thelwall, 1796)

The American painter Washington Allston had first met
Coleridge in Italy, where they became lifelong friends, and his
portrait of 1814 (done in Bristol when Coleridge was forty-two)
presents a large, powerful, suffering man who seems immobilised
in his own dreamy meditations. The plump, round, silver face
above the severe, black clerical garb curiously suggests the full
moon on a dark night, one of Coleridge's enduring images from
'The Ancient Mariner'. Coleridge wrote: 'Whatever is impressive
is part fugitive, part existent only in the imaginations of persons
impressed strongly with my conversation. The face itself is a
FEEBLE, unmanly face ...'. (*Letters*, 1814). Allston's own perceptive
comments are given in the Introduction (see page 26).

Robert Southey (1774 –1843)

History has not been kind to Southey, choosing to forget almost everything he wrote except the famous children's story of *The Three Bears*. Widely admired in his lifetime as a prolific poet, essayist and historian, he was appointed Poet Laureate in 1813, and for thirty years was the most feared and influential critic on the Tory *Quarterly Review*.

Born in Bristol (a lonely child looked after by a rich and eccentric aunt), Southey was educated at Oxford, dreamed of Pantisocracy with Coleridge and wrote revolutionary verse-dramas such as *Wat Tyler* (1794, published 1817), *The Fall of Robespierre* (1794) and *Joan of Arc* (1796), which came back to haunt him in respectable middle age. He spent a formative year in Lisbon, learned Spanish and Portuguese, and returned to marry and settle at Keswick (1803), where he established a huge private library and heroically supported his own and Coleridge's large extended family with regular journalism, translation and reviewing, written to a ferocious daily timetable, with a silver pocket-watch on his desk. In Edward Nash's watercolour of 1820 (page 65) the metamorphosis is complete: revolutionary bard into *Quarterly* reviewer.

The exotic and splendidly titled verse-epics, over which he slaved with such devotion – *Thalaba the Destroyer* (1801), *The Curse of Kehama* (1810), *Roderick: The Last of the Goths* (1814) – were ridiculed by the younger generation. He also had the misfortune to attack both Byron and Shelley in print for their bad poetry

OPPOSITE
Robert Southey
Peter Vandyke, 1795

Robert Southey
Henry Edridge, 1804

and worse morals. Southey retreated into vast histories of Brazil and the Peninsular War, while his sister-in-law hanged herself, and his wife eventually went mad. His best writing is biographical – in remarkably assured lives of Nelson (1813), the preacher John Wesley (1820) and the melancholy poet Cowper (1837) – and in shrewd, funny and refreshingly outspoken letters about his famous friends, especially Lamb, Coleridge, Wordsworth, De Quincey and Walter Scott.

Southey's fine, equine, almost arrogantly handsome face was set on a gangling, long-legged body, giving him something of the appearance of a highly strung, thoroughbred racehorse. Hazlitt recalled him in his youth, before political disillusion and domesticity had curbed him:

> Mr Southey, as we formerly remember to have seen him, had a hectic flush upon his cheek, a roving fire in his eye, a falcon glance, a look at once aspiring and dejected ... .

Robert Southey
Edward Nash, 1820

He wooed Liberty as a youthful lover, but it was perhaps more as a mistress than a bride; and he has since wedded with an elderly and not very reputable lady, called Legitimacy. (*The Spirit of the Age*, 1825)

Many painters called to take his likeness at Keswick, especially after the Laureateship, but Southey disliked most of the results, describing one portrait by Thomas Phillips as giving his eyes 'an expression which I conceive to be more like two oysters in love than anything else.' The drawing by Henry Edridge done in Southey's study in 1804, with Derwentwater and the fells projected like a picturesque backcloth, catches better than most the domesticated bard, well brushed and buttoned up, clever and a touch sarcastic, with elegant socks and shoes that never tramped a hillside. Thomas Carlyle remembered him, 'all legs; in shape and stature like a pair of tongs' (*Reminiscences*, 1881).

Amelia Opie (1769 –1853)

Poet and novelist Amelia Opie (née Alderson) was one of the great beauties of the Romantic generation, entrancing the Godwin circle with her high spirits and revolutionary ardour. The clever daughter of a leading Norwich doctor, well read in French and musically talented, she published her early poems in local papers and sang her own ballads at private receptions.

In 1794 she came to London and attended the treason trials of John Thelwall, Horne Tooke and Thomas Holcroft at the Old Bailey. When Horne Tooke was acquitted, she is said to have walked across the top of the barristers' table to kiss him. She was courted by Holcroft and then Godwin, much to Mary Wollstonecraft's annoyance, but finally married the painter John Opie in 1798. They visited Paris in 1802, after the publication of her *Poems*, which ran to six editions. In 1804 she published her most famous work, *Adeline Mowbray, or The Mother and the Daughter*, a novel about contemporary marriage based partly on the lives of Godwin and Mary Wollstonecraft.

After John Opie's early death in 1807, she returned to Norwich to keep house for her beloved father and became a Quaker, dedicating her life to visiting prisons, hospitals and workhouses. In 1818, however, she said she was still writing for eight hours a day and lamented: 'Shall I ever cease to enjoy the pleasures of this world? I fear not.' Other novels included *Father and Daughter* (1801), *Madeline* (1822) and the unfinished *The Painter and His Wife*. She kept up a wide circle of friends in both London and Paris, including Byron, Scott, Wordsworth, Madame de Staël and Lafayette. When she died a street was named after her in Norwich.

Amelia Opie
John Opie, 1798

With her large brown eyes, clear bold features and voluptuous figure, Mrs Opie always attracted clever men and alarmed clever women. Crabb Robinson noted that 'her becoming a Quakeress gave her a sort of éclat' (*Diary*, 1824); Mrs Inchbald called her 'cleverer than her books'; while Miss Sedgwick cattily observed that her 'elaborate simplicity and the fashionable little train to her pretty satin gown indicated how much easier it is to adopt a theory than to change one's habits' (*Letters from Abroad*, 1840).

John Opie's portrait is a tender tribute to his wife, painted in the year of their marriage. Its intimacy is emphasised by the direct unflinching gaze (with its hint of mischief), the fullness of the mouth and the casual placing of the formal hat with its riding veil on her knee. The beautifully braided hair subtly suggests a laurel wreath, symbol of literary renown.

William Hazlitt (1778 –1830)

Political journalist and superb all-round critic of the arts, Hazlitt became the radical conscience of Romanticism. Famed equally for the gusto of his prose and the bitterness of his quarrels, he was a lifelong republican. The son of a Unitarian preacher from Ireland, Hazlitt first trained for the Dissenting ministry and then as a portrait-painter, but, inspired by a meeting with Coleridge and Wordsworth in the Quantocks in 1798, he gradually took up freelance writing. This experience is memorably described in one of his greatest essays, *My First Acquaintance with Poets* (1823).

Hazlitt could write with equal brilliance on theatre, painting, boxing, politics, poetry and long-distance walking. Keats said that 'the depth of Hazlitt's taste' was one of the three glories of the age (the other two being Wordsworth's poetry and Haydon's pictures). His major essays were collected in *The Characters of Shakespeare's Plays* (1817), *Political Essays* (1819), *Lectures on The English Comic Writers* (1819) and *Winterslow* (1831), named after his writing retreat on the edge of Salisbury Plain. He produced a vivid and often devastating assessment of his contemporaries in a gallery of twenty-five pen portraits (including Coleridge, Wordsworth, Southey, Godwin, Byron and Scott) collected as *The Spirit of the Age* (1825).

Lonely and mercurial, he was twice married (both times unhappily), and in 1823 published *Liber Amoris*, the agonised account of his unrequited passion for Sarah Walker, a teenage servant girl. His conversations with the painter James Northcote, an interesting experiment in biography, were collected as *Boswell Redivivus* (1827). Hazlitt ended his days in tragic isolation and

William Hazlitt
William Bewick, 1825
Coleridge, whom Hazlitt both praised and mocked, gave this memorable verbal portrait of Hazlitt at twenty-four: 'William Hazlitt is a thinking, observant, original man … . His manners are to 99 in 100 singularly repulsive – brow-hanging, shoe-contemplative, strange … he is, I verily believe, kindly-natured … but he is jealous, gloomy, & of an irritable Pride – & addicted to women, as objects of sexual Indulgence. With all this there is much good in him … he says things that are his own in a way of his own … he sends well-headed & well-feathered Thoughts straight forwards to the mark with a Twang of the Bow-string' (*Letters*, 1802).

poverty, working on a four-volume life of his hero, Napoleon, and sending a last letter to the editor of the *Edinburgh Review* from his Soho lodgings: 'Dear Sir, I am dying; can you send me £10, and so consummate your many kindnesses to me?' (*Letters*, 1830). Hazlitt's extraordinary mixture of shyness and aggression was not easily captured on canvas. The Bewick sketch (above) was done during his second honeymoon at Melrose in Scotland, and his wife remarked: 'Oh, it is exactly your own hair, my dear' (T. Landseer, *Life of Bewick*, 1871). Some years later, his friend George Patmore recalled him as 'a pale anatomy of a man … the forehead was magnificent, the nose strong, light and elegant, the mouth greatly resembled Edmund Kean's, the eyes grey (furtive), sometimes sinister, never brilliant, the head nobly formed with a profusion of coal-black curls' (*My Friends and Acquaintances*, 1854).

Charles Lamb (1775 –1834)

The most kind and lovable of men, Lamb set out to be a poet but found his true identity as an essayist and whimsical autobiographer. He created the persona of 'Elia', who could enliven any subject under the sun, from reading Shakespeare to eating roast pig for supper. The son of a lawyer's clerk of the Inner Temple, Lamb attended Christ's Hospital School with Coleridge, and then worked for forty years as a clerk in the East India Company in the City.

Almost all Lamb's work is a celebration of London and the metropolitan sensibility, just as his closest friends celebrated the Lake District and wild nature. One of his most penetrating early essays was *On the Genius and Character of Hogarth* (1811). His occasional poems, tender and elegiac, include 'The Old Familiar Faces' (1798), the ballad 'Hester' (1803), and the infinitely touching 'On an Infant Dying as Soon as Born' (1827).

Insanity dogged Lamb's family: Lamb himself spent six weeks in Hoxton Lunatic Asylum in 1795, and the following year his beloved elder sister Mary was incarcerated there for five months after fatally stabbing their mother during a paranoid episode. Lamb dedicated the rest of his life to looking after Mary, and together they published *Tales from Shakespeare* (1807) and *Adventures of Ulysses* (1808) for children. His rooms near the Strand became the late-night meeting place for his many friends, including Coleridge, Wordsworth, Southey, Hazlitt, Haydon and Leigh Hunt. Here Lamb presided in a celestial cloud of tobacco smoke, port fumes and precipitate puns, brought to earth with his inimitable stutter. The first collected volume of the *Essays of Elia*, dedicated to Coleridge, appeared in 1823, and the second

Charles Lamb
William Hazlitt, 1804

in 1833. When he died Wordsworth mourned him in a poem as 'Lamb, the frolic and the gentle'.

Small, animated, deeply eccentric and often rather drunk, no painter ever captured Lamb's pixie-like and mischievous charm. He had one brown eye and one grey. His reply to Coleridge's loving epithet, 'my gentle-hearted Charles' (in the poem 'This Lime-Tree Bower My Prison'), was characteristic: 'call me rather drunken-dog, ragged head, seldom-shaven, odd-ey'd, stuttering, or any other epithet which truly and properly belongs' (*Letters*, 1797). He got his own back twenty

years later by calling Coleridge, in a superb phrase, 'an Archangel
a little Damaged' (*Letters*, 1816). Leigh Hunt wrote: 'Charles Lamb
had a head worthy of Aristotle, with as fine a heart as ever beat
in a human bosom, and limbs very fragile to sustain it ... . There
never was a true portrait of Lamb' (*Autobiography*, 1850).

The best attempt is Hazlitt's curiously solemn picture of
1804, one of the last he ever painted before taking up writing,
which Crabb Robinson drily described as 'certainly the only
painting by Hazlitt that I ever saw with pleasure' (*Diary*, 1812).
The seventeenth-century Spanish costume was not the result of
Lamb dressing up (like Byron in Albanian draperies) for theatrical
effect as an Iberian Elia. It was instead a typical act of lambent
friendship: Hazlitt wanted to do a copy of Velázquez's *Philip IV*,
and Lamb had humbly agreed to act as his clothes-horse. One
can only imagine the philippic puns that accompanied the sitting.

Mary Robinson (1758–1800)

Poet, actress, novelist and adventuress, Mary 'Perdita' Robinson was one of the most glamorous and talented women of her generation, embodying the early spirit of Romanticism in her life as much as her work. She played many of Shakespeare's heroines in the London theatres between 1778 and 1790, and in the last decade of her career published seven novels and three volumes of poetry. She knew Godwin and befriended the young Coleridge, hearing him recite 'Kubla Khan' sixteen years before the poem was published. She was poetry editor of *The Morning Post*, and probably influenced the narrative style of the *Lyrical Ballads* (1798).

Married at sixteen to a feckless husband (with whom she spent ten months in prison for debt), Mary Robinson took to the stage and caught the eye of the teenage Prince of Wales while

Mary Robinson
by or after Sir Joshua Reynolds, c.1782

playing Perdita in *The Winter's Tale* at Covent Garden in 1779. After a heady year as the royal mistress (from whence her nickname), she moved into the bed of the great Opposition statesman Charles James Fox, who arranged for her to receive a state pension of £500 per annum, a considerable sum giving her complete independence, and then formed a passionate but fraught alliance with a distinguished military historian and MP, the roving Colonel Tarleton, which lasted on and off till the end of her life.

In 1792 she visited revolutionary France, in the middle of a lover's quarrel. But a near-fatal miscarriage left her increasingly paralysed with an agonising form of arthritis and, in her remarkable *Memoirs* (published posthumously in 1801), she describes how she took opium against the pain and wrote under its influence in a way very similar to Coleridge. While her novels are sentimental, her poetry has unexpected dash and clarity. Very much in her own voice, it is sometimes racily satirical, but always stylish.

Like the other Romantics, she made poetry out of the incidents of her own life, but also identified very early on the subjects that would attract her male contemporaries. Her *Poems* (1791) include an 'Ode to Melancholy' and an 'Ode to the Nightingale', as well as 'Monody to the Memory of Chatterton' and 'Sonnet: the Mariner'. In the year of her death, Coleridge wrote her a touching poem of greeting and farewell, 'A Stranger Minstrel', praising her 'witching melody'.

Famous for her imperious beauty (as well as her dramatic hats), Mary Robinson was frequently painted by Romney,

Mary Robinson
George Dance, 1793

Gainsborough, Reynolds and Zoffany. But for them she was primarily an actress on display. George Dance's intimate, rather melancholy drawing, done in later life (1793), shows her instead as a writer more at home in her private study, wrapped up in a plain day dress with her hair pulled back in a practical – but typically flamboyant – silk scarf with its seductive bow.

Almost her last publication was a spirited essay in support of Mary Wollstonecraft, *A Letter to the Women of England on the Injustice of Mental Subordination* (1799), in which she recommended the foundation of a University for Women.

Edmund Kean (1787–1833)

A tragic actor of unnerving power, Kean brought a new sense of psychological depth to the English stage. Small, dark and intense, he could instantly dominate an audience with his brilliant eyes, and became famous for his reinterpretation of Shakespeare's villains and outsiders. Hazlitt wrote that he destroyed for ever 'the Kemble religion' of classical acting.

Born in London, unstable and probably illegitimate (his Jewish father flung himself off a roof), Kean learned his craft in travelling circuses and fairground booths, often playing Hamlet and Harlequin on the same night. His debut as Shylock at the Drury Lane Theatre in January 1814 took London by storm.

Edmund Kean as Richard III
J. Prynn, c.1814–33

It was followed over the next decade by redefining performances of Richard III, Othello, Iago, Hamlet and King Lear. His brooding, volatile manner on stage, combined with his radical politics and disreputable private life ('Give me bread and cheese and a couple of whores!' he shouted at his manager, Elliston), earned him a Mephistophelean reputation. Byron (a member of the Drury Lane Committee) said approvingly that Kean was like his own Corsair and had 'a laughing devil in his sneer'.

Kean undertook two successful American tours (there were riots in Boston and New York) and was made an honorary Huron chieftain. Back in London he sometimes received guests in feathers and warpaint. He purchased a large house in Piccadilly and an island estate in Scotland, and triumphantly sent his son to Eton. But venereal disease, alcohol and a scandalous trial for adultery forced him into early retirement in Richmond (after three 'final' benefit nights). Walter Scott drily observed that Kean was 'rendered mad by conceit and success', but for Coleridge Kean's stage performances were 'like reading Shakespeare by flashes of lightning' (*Shakespearean Criticism*, 1840).

OPPOSITE
Edmund Kean as Shylock
Henry Hoppner Meyer; W.H. Watts, 1814

Dorothy Jordan (1761–1816)

Exuberant Yorkshire actress and singer renowned for her unruly mop of auburn curls, Dora Jordan began her career in Dublin playing Miss Lucy in Fielding's comedy *The Virgin Unmasked* and ended it in London playing royal mistress to the Duke of Clarence, later William IV. Mrs Jordan (the stage name she adopted because she had successfully 'crossed over the waters') became the most celebrated romantic comedy actress of her generation and was painted by Hoppner for the Royal Academy as *The Comic Muse* (1786).

Her seductive cross-dressing parts, which included Viola in *Twelfth Night*, Rosalind in *As You Like It* and Priscilla Tomboy in *The Romp*, brought her a huge following, including Lamb, Hazlitt, Hunt, Coleridge, Fanny Burney and even Jane Austen (who was 'highly amused' watching her at Covent Garden in 1814). At the height of 'Jordo-mania', Beechey painted her in skin-tight yellow knee breeches (1789) and Hoppner in the peacock uniform of a Spanish hussar (1791). Her tender, flirtatious acting style brought a new Romantic poignancy to Shakespeare's heroines, especially Juliet, Miranda and Ophelia, and made the classical solemnity of Sarah Siddons suddenly old-fashioned.

Lamb described her succinctly as 'Shakespeare's

Mrs Jordan as Viola .

Dorothy Jordan
John Hoppner, exhibited 1791
According to Hazlitt: 'her face, her tears, her manners were irresistible ... . She was all gaiety, openness and good nature. She rioted in fine animal spirits, and gave more pleasure than any other actress, because she had the greatest spirit of enjoyment in herself' (*View of the English Stage*, 1818).

woman'. From 1791 she was also the Duke's mistress and bore him no fewer than ten children, skilfully alternating pregnancies with stage appearances. Their domestic *ménage* became the subject of endlessly suggestive cartoons by Gillray, many punning on her stage name ('jordan' being Regency slang for 'chamberpot'). Comedy finally turned to tragedy when the Duke cast her off in 1811, making an allowance with the cruel proviso that she could not act again. She fled to France as 'Mrs James', where she died at Saint-Cloud, heartbroken and penniless. But she was never forgotten by her true Romantic devotees.

OPPOSITE
Dorothy Jordan as Viola
Unknown artist, late eighteenth century

Thomas De Quincey
Sir John Watson-Gordon, c.1845

Thomas De Quincey (1785 –1859)

The strangest and most exotic of the Romantics, De Quincey made his name at the age of thirty-seven with his *Confessions of an English Opium Eater* (1821), written in a garret off Covent Garden and originally published the previous year in two instalments by the *London Magazine*. Scholarly, fantastical, deeply read in German and Oriental literature, De Quincey was a gentleman bohemian who supported himself, a large family and his lifelong drug-addiction by a huge output of journalism. He became the master of a baroque form of autobiographical dream-prose and a critic of peculiar psychological insights. His taste for the grotesque and his combination of arcane learning with black humour are brilliantly displayed in his essays *On Murder Considered as One of the Fine Arts* (1827) and *On the Knocking on the Gate in Macbeth* (1823).

The son of a wealthy linen merchant, eccentric in his habits and diminutive in stature (he was barely five feet tall), De Quincey absconded first from Manchester Grammar School and then from Oxford, drifting through Wales and London, reading the poetry of Wordsworth and Coleridge, taking opium and living with a teenage prostitute whom he tenderly describes in his *Confessions* as 'Ann of Oxford Street'. In 1808 he settled in the Lake District near his idol Wordsworth, taking over Dove Cottage and filling it with fifty-six tea chests of books.

De Quincey's memories of this time, shrewd and mischievous, later appeared as *Recollections of the Lake Poets* (1834–9) with memorable portraits of William and Dorothy Wordsworth, Coleridge and Southey. He lived with the daughter of a local farmer, whom he finally married in 1817, producing eight children. Thereafter he drifted between London and Edinburgh, writing irregular but brilliant essays in his 'impassioned prose', including an unfinished study of his opium-dreams, *Suspiria de Profundis* (1845, *Sighs from the Deep*), and the thrilling, moonlit vision of disaster entitled *The English Mail Coach* (1849). His work made an immediate impact in France, second only to Byron's, and was translated by Baudelaire in *Les Paradis Artificiels*, and praised by Gautier.

When De Quincey first came to Grasmere, Dorothy Wordsworth was entranced by his ability to play with the children and he always retained an impish, changeling quality, as if his whole life was some fantastic, labyrinthian game. 'We feel often as if he were one of the Family – he is loving, gentle and happy – a very good scholar, and an acute Logician … . His person is unfortunately *diminutive*, but there is a sweetness in his looks, especially about the eyes, which soon overcomes the oddness in your first feeling at the sight of so very little a Man' (*Letters*, 1808).

In later life, when opium and poverty had taken their toll, Crabb Robinson observed a pale, wizened creature whose strangeness was nonetheless still attractive: 'In London he could not possibly maintain himself. I saw him occasionally there as a shiftless man. He had a wretchedly invalid countenance: his skin looked like mother-of-pearl. He had a very delicate hand & voice more soft than a woman's, but his conversation was highly intelligent and interesting' (*Reminiscences*, 1843). Sir John Watson-Gordon's portrait was done at about this time (*c*.1845). The large, heavy, handsome overcoat with its furred collar and sleeves seems deliberately designed to disguise the shrunken, penniless, haunted Opium Eater within.

Sir William Herschel (1738–1822)

Astronomer and cosmologist of visionary genius, Herschel revolutionised Romantic ideas about the size and nature of the physical universe.

Born into a family of German musicians, he emigrated to England and in 1767 settled in Bath, where he was employed as an organist and music teacher. Increasingly drawn by the music of the spheres, he built a series of reflector telescopes in his back garden, hand-grinding their enormous mirrors and spending entire nights mapping the constellations. In March 1781 he observed a strange comet in Taurus, which turned out to be the seventh planet in the solar system, Uranus, the first to be discovered since the time of Ptolemy. For this he was knighted, appointed royal astronomer and later celebrated

William Herschel
Lemuel Francis Abbott, 1785

by Keats in his sonnet 'On First Looking into Chapman's Homer' (1816).

Herschel established a giant forty-foot telescope near Windsor and began to formulate startling new theories about evolving galaxies *beyond* the Milky Way ('On the Construction of the Heavens', 1785) and the existence of 'deep time'. He was also romantic enough to believe that the moon was inhabited.

Shelley discussed his cosmology in the 'Notes' to *Queen Mab* (1811); Byron reflected gloomily that 'Night was a more religious concern' when observed through Herschel's telescope (*Detached Thoughts*, 1821), while Fanny Burney exclaimed wildly that Herschel had discovered 'fifteen hundred universes! How many more he may find who can conjecture?' (*Diary*, December 1786).

He told the poet Thomas Campbell: 'I have looked further into space than ever human being did before me. I have observed stars of which the light, it can be proved, must take two million years to reach the earth.' In response, Campbell remarked that '... anything you ask he labours to explain with a sort of boyish earnestness ... . I really and unfeignedly felt at the moment as if I had been conversing with a supernatural intelligence.' (Letter, September 1815)

Caroline Herschel, his beloved younger sister, discovered several new comets. She went on to become the first woman scientist elected to the Astronomical Society and receive a royal stipend. It was she who chose Herschel's epitaph: 'He burst the bounds of Heaven.'

William Herschel
James Godby, published 1814

Sir Humphry Davy (1778–1829)

The greatest British scientist of his day and President of the Royal Society, Davy was also an intimate friend of Coleridge and Wordsworth, knew Scott and Byron, and was a gifted minor poet in his own right. He published a delightful volume of piscatorial reflections (in dialogue form), *Salmonia, or Days of Fly-Fishing* (1828), and a moving book of meditations, *Consolations in Travel, or the Last Days of a Philosopher* (1830). His brilliant career shows no evidence of the modern split between the 'two cultures', and his ability to explain and popularise his experimental work in books and lectures (which particularly influenced Coleridge) suggests that there was once such a thing as Romantic science. He wrote: 'Whilst chemical pursuits exalt the understanding, they do not depress the imagination or weaken genuine feeling.'

A Cornishman by birth, Davy researched at the famous Bristol Pneumatic Institution under Dr Thomas Beddoes (where Coleridge joined him in experiments with laughing gas) and oversaw the proof corrections to the *Lyrical Ballads*. In 1803 he was appointed Professor of Chemistry at the newly founded Royal Institution in London, and began his celebrated Bakerian Lectures at the Royal Society, demonstrating the electrical affinity of chemical elements and isolating sodium and potassium. Like a true Romantic, he had an instinctive appreciation of fire and combustion, inventing in 1813 the famous Davy Safety Lamp, an 'insulated light' which did not ignite the lethal hydrogen

....
OPPOSITE
Sir Humphry Davy
Thomas Phillips, 1821

or methane gases in deep-pit mine shafts. Another of his more hazardous experiments was to launch Coleridge as a lecturer at the Royal Institution in 1808.

In 1812 he was knighted for his work, and received many other honours both in London and in Paris. However, his marriage of the same year to a fashionable Scottish blue-stocking, Jane Apreece, was childless and increasingly discordant. By the time he was appointed President of the Royal Society (1820), he had become an isolated and tragically embittered man, cut off from his friends, gloomy and introspective, and suffering from progressive heart disease.

....

Scientific researches! – new discoveries in pneumaticks!
James Gillray, 1802
A mixed audience at the Royal Institution observes the startling effects of inhaling nitrous oxide, or laughing gas, administered by Professor Young and a leering Humphry Davy (with bellows).

His great protégé, Michael Faraday, found him cold and remote. Davy travelled much on the Continent, drinking, fly-fishing and writing (like Coleridge and Shelley he produced a long poem on 'Mont Blanc'), and died in a hotel room in Geneva aged fifty. But he left the Romantics with a noble and dynamic view of the physical universe as a constant flux of energies and mysterious forms.

An attractive, rather boyish figure with dark Celtic features and a commanding nose, Davy burst into life on the lecture platform and had the gift of enchanting his audiences. 'He is now about thirty-three,' wrote George Ticknor in 1815, 'but with all the freshness and bloom of five-and-twenty, and one of the handsomest men I have seen in England' (*Life and Letters*, 1876). Phillips's portrait was executed after a miners' banquet held in Davy's honour at Newcastle and shows the elegant shape of the Davy Lamp, which saved so many of their lives, placed proudly at his elbow.

Lord Byron (1788–1824)

With Lord Byron, English Romanticism developed into an international style. A charismatic figure of devastating charm and vanity, Byron became the *beau ideal* of the Romantic writer while pretending to do nothing so unspeakably vulgar. His poems were effortless best-sellers, his letters are among the finest and funniest in the language, and his stormy private life inspired over two hundred biographies and memoirs. His masterpiece is *Don Juan*, an autobiographical poem in five cantos begun in 1818, which reflects his lifelong travels through Europe and the Levant, and is written in his wonderful world-weary style of mocking colloquialisms and lyric irony.

His father, 'Mad Jack' Byron, died when he was only three and Byron grew up at Newstead Abbey, a dilapidated gothic pile in Nottinghamshire, a clever, lonely and passionate child who was always haunted by a secret 'mark of Cain', his club foot. At Cambridge he formed a brilliant circle of dandyish friends (one of them, Scrope Davies, noted that he slept in paper curlers) and in 1809 he set the literary establishment on fire with his satire 'English Bards and Scotch Reviewers'.

He came back from two years' wanderings in Spain, Malta, Greece and Turkey to publish the first two cantos of *Childe Harold's Pilgrimage* (1812) and 'awoke to find myself famous'. These were followed by several Oriental verse-tales (*The Corsair* was written in ten days) and a glorious period of social lionising, including his scandalous affair with the volatile Lady Caroline Lamb (1785–1828), who sometimes dressed for him as a pageboy.

Lady Caroline Lamb subsequently published a gothic novel of her passionate entanglement with Byron, *Glenarvon* (1816), and died insane twelve years later.

Lord Byron
Thomas Phillips, c.1835, after the portrait of 1813

Byron worked for the Drury Lane Theatre Committee, made lasting alliances with Walter Scott and the poet Tom Moore (a future biographer, 1830) and encouraged Coleridge to publish 'Christabel'. But the liaison with his half-sister, Augusta Leigh, and the collapse of his marriage to Arabella Millbank drove him abroad again in 1816, to settle in Italy with his menagerie of Venetian mistresses and exotic animals, brilliantly evoked in his poem 'Beppo' (1818). In 1821 he moved to the Palazzo Lanfranchi, Pisa, with the Countess Teresa Guiccioli, a bulldog and a billiard table.

His magnetic presence attracted Shelley and his wife, Mary (whose half-sister Claire Clairmont became another mistress), and innumerable raffish admirers and hangers-on. Among these were the young Scottish physician John William Polidori (1795–1821), author of *The Vampyre* (1819), who later committed suicide. Most striking was Edward John Trelawny (1792–1881), a bearded Cornish adventurer and inspired teller of tall stories who cast himself as a natural Byronic hero and in 1822 accompanied Byron to the Greek War of Independence. His *Records of Shelley, Byron and the Author* (1858) is a vividly convincing and totally unreliable work of Romantic biography.

Byron's final commitment to the Philhellene cause in Greece electrified the youth of Europe and hundreds rushed to join him. His private disillusion in the brutal chaos of the war, witnessed in his last letters and poems ('Tis time this heart should be unmoved', dated Missolonghi, 22 January 1824), was offset by extraordinary courage and generosity, and an unflinching dedication to 'Freedom's battle'. Stylish and self-mocking to the end (he sported a plumed helmet but lamented the grey hairs beneath), his death from fever at Missolonghi in April 1824 was mourned throughout Europe and signalled the apotheosis of Romanticism. In Lincolnshire, on hearing the news, a young poet called Tennyson carved 'Byron is Dead' upon a rock.

Byron's fine aristocratic beauty was admired equally by men and women, and inspired dozens of pictures, sketches,

OPPOSITE FROM LEFT TO RIGHT
Lady Caroline Lamb
Henry Hoppner Meyer,
published 1819

Edward John Trelawny
Joseph Severn, 1838

LEFT
John William Polidori
F.G. Gainsford, c.1816

Lord Byron
E.H. Bailey, 1826

busts and medallions both during his lifetime and after. The large head with its dark curls, mocking eyes and voluptuous mouth, distracted from the stocky body that was always tending to overweight and the distinctive limp with its hint of the cloven hoof. He was Apollo combined with Mephistopheles.

'Lord Byron's head,' wrote John Gibson Lockhart, 'is without doubt the finest in our time – I think it better on the whole, than either Napoleon's, or Goethe's, or Canova's, or Wordsworth's' (*Letters*, 1819). Byron himself was typically droll on the matter: 'my personal charms have by no means increased – my hair is half grey – and the Crow's foot has been rather lavish of its indelible steps – my hair though not gone is going – and my teeth remain by way of courtesy – but I suppose they will follow' (*Letters*, 1819). But Coleridge recalled that being in Byron's presence was like seeing the sun (*Letters*, 1816).

Sir Walter Scott (1771–1832)

Now remembered as a great historical novelist, Scott first made his name as a poet and prolific writer of Romantic verse-tales. He had no reputation as a novelist until his mid-forties, and his work was seen primarily as a rival to Southey's and Byron's. Fascinated by the Border ballads of his native Lowlands and a skilful translator of German gothic ballads by Bürger and Goethe (which also attracted Coleridge and Wordsworth), he published *Minstrelsy of the Scottish Borders* in 1802–3.

Scott popularised a form of highly musical, melodramatic, 'antiquarian' verse-tales of the Highlands – battles, hauntings, castles, lakes and star-crossed lovers – whose titles still hold an

ineffable misty romance: *The Lay of the Last Minstrel* (1805), *The Lady of the Lake* (1810), *The Bridal of Triermain* (1813) and *The Lord of the Isles* (1815). It was only when his audience was finally captured by Byron that he turned to prose and the vast resources of Scottish clan history. Among his outstanding achievements were the original *Waverley* (1814), *Old Mortality* (1816), *Rob Roy* (1817), *The Heart of Midlothian* (1817), *Ivanhoe* (1819), *Quentin Durward* (1823) and *Castle Dangerous* (1831).

Sir Walter Scott
Augustin Edouart, 1830–1

As the author of such wild and aboriginal romances, Scott's solid, genial and meticulous nature presents a curious paradox. He was educated at Edinburgh University, successfully trained for the Scottish bar, became a partner in Ballantyne's publishing house, helped found the *Quarterly Review* and took immense pride in his manse at Abbotsford on the Tweed, which he purchased in 1811. He was Sheriff-depute of Selkirkshire and was knighted in 1820. It was wholly characteristic that he refused the Poet Laureateship (in Southey's favour) in 1813, and when Ballantyne's went bankrupt in 1826 he shouldered the huge debt of £114, 000 and gradually paid it off from the profits of his pen – a heroic effort which undoubtedly shortened his life. The one shadow in his career was that he was accused, with some reason, of plagiarising Coleridge's 'Christabel' in his early work, but this could be taken as a compliment.

Gruff, witty, hospitable, hard-working and hard-drinking – every inch a Scotsman – Scott was often painted in his lair at Abbotsford. 'There was more benevolence expressed in Scott's face,' said his friend the painter C.R. Leslie, 'than is given in any portrait of him' (*Autobiographical Recollections*, 1865). But the fine florid, distinguished features – with hair prematurely silver – and tall, powerful body all spoke clearly of his inner strength and creative force.

Sir Walter Scott
Sir Edwin Landseer, c.1824
Landseer went up to paint this portrait at Abbotsford in 1824, while Scott was working on Redgauntlet.
'He has painted every dog in the house,' remarked Scott, 'and ended up with the owner' (*Letters*, 1824).

Percy Bysshe Shelley (1792–1822)

As reckless and brilliant in his poetry as in his life, Shelley poured out the great body of his major work in less than a decade, and drowned (with two friends) off the coast of Tuscany at the age of twenty-nine, while trying to race a summer storm back to Lerici in his small yacht and pressing on with full sail. He is still popularly remembered as a love poet ('Lines Written in the Bay of Lerici'), a master of plangent lyrics ('To a Skylark'), of superb odes ('To the West Wind') and moving elegies ('Adonais', on the death of Keats). But he was also a philosophical and political essayist, and a gifted poetic translator from German, Italian, Greek, Spanish and Arabic.

Many of Shelley's radical and revolutionary ideas, powerfully influenced by his father-in-law William Godwin, were expressed in his great dramatic poem *Prometheus Unbound* (1820). He wrote wonderful letters about his travels in Italy, describing it as 'the Paradise of Exiles', and a historic *Defence of Poetry* (1821). Wordsworth called him 'one of the best artists of us all; I mean in workmanship of style.'

The rebellious son of a Sussex baronet, Shelley was educated at Eton and Oxford (from which he was sent down for atheism), and was twice married. His first wife, Harriet Westbrook, committed suicide in the Serpentine; his second wife, Mary Godwin, wrote *Frankenstein*; and two of his children died in Italy. His complex relationship with Byron is described in one of his finest, plainest and most haunting poems, 'Julian and Maddalo' (1818). At the time of his death, while living at his remote beach-house, the Casa Magni in San Terenzo, Shelley was working on a long poem in *terza rima* based on Dante's

Percy Bysshe Shelley
Amelia Curran, 1819

Inferno, the visionary 'Triumph of Life'. Parts of this manuscript
are written on the back of drawings of the sailing rig for his
yacht, the *Don Juan*.

His friend Thomas Love Peacock (1785–1866) affectionately
satirised him – along with Byron and Coleridge – as the unworldly
idealist Scythrop Glowry in the novel *Nightmare Abbey* (1818).
Thin, wide-eyed and intense, Shelley was an expert pistol shot,
a good horse-rider, an athletic walker and a convinced
vegetarian. Impetuous by temperament and much troubled
by physical seizures (probably kidney stones) and psychic
manifestations, he lived with an unsettling urgency that affected
all those around him. His sensible banker friend Horace Smith
called him 'a psychological curiosity, infinitely more curious
than Coleridge's Kubla Khan'. (Letter, 1816)

The only authentic portrait of Shelley was painted by
Amelia Curran in her studio near the Spanish Steps in Rome,
at the time he was finishing *Prometheus Unbound* in 1819. Curran

Thomas Love Peacock
Roger Jean, c.1805

later told Mary Shelley that she had almost burned the picture, because it was 'so ill done' and had failed to capture his restless spirit. Leigh Hunt, who saw Shelley in the port of Livorno a few days before he drowned, left a memorable description:

His figure was tall and slight, and his constitution consumptive. He was subject to violent spasmodic pains ... his shoulders were bent a little, owing to premature thought and trouble ... . Like the Stagyrite's, his voice was high and weak. His eyes were large and animated, with a dash of wildness in them ... . He had brown hair, which, though tinged with grey, surmounted his face well, being in considerable quantity, and tending to curl ... when fronting and looking at you attentively his aspect had a certain seraphical character that would have suited a portrait of John the Baptist, or the angel whom Milton describes as holding a reed 'tipt' with fire. (*Autobiography*, 1850)

Mary Shelley (1797–1851)

Celebrated as the author of one unforgettable book, *Frankenstein, or The Modern Prometheus*, which was published when she was twenty-one, Mary Shelley was actually a professional *femme de lettres* of many talents and striking versatility. She wrote six major novels, over forty short stories, a travel book (based on her Continental adventures with Shelley) and numerous essays and short biographies. She also produced an autobiographical novella of her mental breakdown in Italy, *Mathilda* (1819), and a confessional poem about her life after Shelley's death, 'The Choice' (1822) – both unpublished until the twentieth century – as well as the moving biographical 'Notes' to the 1839 edition of Shelley's *Collected Poems*.

The beautiful only child of William Godwin and Mary Wollstonecraft (who died in childbirth), she was her father's darling and was privately educated to a standard far higher than usually achieved at Oxford or at Cambridge (Girton, the first college for women, was not founded until 1869). After her elopement with Shelley in 1814 (which shattered Godwin as much as her mother's death had sixteen years previously), she published her first book anonymously, *History of a Six Weeks Tour* (1817), in collaboration with Shelley.

Frankenstein, also anonymous, followed in 1818, on the eve of their departure for Italy. Inspired by a ghost-story competition with Byron and Polidori at the Villa Diodati, Lake Geneva, in the summer of 1816, it broke the conventions of the eighteenth-century gothic novel to become the first recognisable work of modern science fiction. Its celebrated 'eight foot' monster (subsequently the star of a score of modern films,

Mary Shelley
Richard Rothwell,
exhibited 1840

of which the best by far was Kenneth Branagh's in 1994) is as much a Romantic outcast, a sort of Adam after the Fall, as a Hammer House horror figure with a bolt through his neck. Much of Mary's own scientific reading about electrical phenomena and anatomy, as well as her own terrible experiences in childbirth, went into the book; and it has been convincingly argued that Dr Frankenstein is a composite portrait of both her father and her husband. After the trauma of Shelley's death, Mary returned to London in 1823 (where *Frankenstein* was already being staged) to look after her father and her surviving son, Percy Florence.

Though much courted (by women as well as men), she never remarried but lived quietly in retirement, steadily publishing her later novels: *Valperga* (1823), *The Last Man* (1826,

also a science fiction novel set in a republican England in
the twenty-first century), *The Fortunes of Perkin Warbeck* (1830,
a historical romance), *Lodore* (1835), *Falkner* (1837) and a
distinguished biographical collection, *Lives of the Most Eminent
Literary and Scientific Men of France* (1837). She sent her son to
Harrow, like Byron, and dedicated the remainder of her life
to seeing him conventionally educated, happily married
and safely settled on his country estate at Boscombe Down,
Sussex, to be as much unlike his father as possible.

Brilliantly clever, shy, pale and painfully unexpressive in
company, Mary Shelley hid a passionate nature that probably
very few people except Godwin, Shelley and her friend Jane
Williams (whose husband was also drowned in the yacht disaster)
ever really saw. Her half-sister, Claire Clairmont, called her
'a mixture of vanity and good nature'.

Her elusive character is oddly reflected in the history of
her portraits. An early picture by Amelia Curran done in Rome
(1819) was lent to Trelawny for safe-keeping and subsequently
lost in his wanderings. Drawings by Edward Williams done at
Pisa for Shelley's birthday (1821) disappeared after the shipwreck.
A striking portrait of 'an unknown woman' by John Stump
(National Portrait Gallery, 1831), said to be Mary surrounded
by her books and holding up a lover's locket assumed to contain
Shelley's hair, has been consistently dismissed by modern art
historians as unauthenticated, even though it corresponds
closely to a contemporary description by Elizabeth Rennie:

> If not a beauty, she was a most lovable-looking woman;
> with skin exquisitely fair, and expressive gray eyes; features
> delicate, yet of the style and proportion that have won the

Frontispiece to *Frankenstein*, (3rd edition)
W. Chevalier after T. Holst, 1831

term 'aristocratic'; hair of light but bright brown, mostly silky in texture and luxuriant in profusion, which hung in long drooping ringlets over her colourless cheek, and gathered in a cluster behind, fell waveringly over her shoulders; a large, open forehead; white and well-moulded arms and hands. She was a degree under the middle height, and rather enclining to embonpoint. (*Traits of Character*, Vol. 1, 1860)

Richard Rothwell's portrait, showing Mary as a much-subdued and evidently suffering older woman, was probably completed in 1840. Though the eyes are still full of tender intelligence, the great 'alabaster' shoulders suggest that she is turning into a monument. The curious 'flame-like' drapery in the background, revealed during cleaning at the turn of the century, was said to represent Shelley's unappeased spirit awaiting their reunion.

Leigh Hunt (1784–1859)

Literary journalist, essayist and gifted verse-writer, Hunt proved himself a brilliant and courageous campaigning editor of the *The Examiner* (1808–21). With his brother John as business manager, he made it the outstanding liberal Sunday newspaper of the Romantic period, renowned for its new poetry, its generous reviewing and its reformist politics.

Imprisoned from 1813 to 1815 for seditious libel against the Prince Regent ('this fat Adonis'), Hunt characteristically transformed his grim prison cell into a dilettante's 'bower of bliss', complete with grand piano, classical busts, rose-patterned wallpaper and painted sky-blue ceiling. Here he became the object of literary pilgrimage, visited by Byron, Moore, Hazlitt, Haydon and Lamb. In December 1816 he began the celebrated 'Young Poets' series, which launched the careers of Keats and Shelley. Mocked as patron of the 'Cockney School of Poetry' (Lockhart, *Blackwood's Magazine*, 1817), he still had considerable success with his own decorative and beguiling verse, *The Story of Rimini* (1816), based on Dante's erotic tale of Paolo and Francesca. In 1821 he sailed to Italy to launch *The Liberal*, but was devastated when he quickly lost its main contributors, Shelley (drowned) and Byron (struck down by fever in Greece), though he published work by Hazlitt and Mary Shelley. Hunt returned to edit further magazines (*The Companion*, *The Tatler*) and pleasing anthologies (*The Book of Gems*), but was doomed to live in the posthumous shadow of his more famous friends, publishing a provocative memoir, *Lord Byron and Some of his Contemporaries*, in 1828 and much later his shrewd and revealing *Autobiography* (1850), which contains a moving portrait of Shelley (page 101).

James Henry Leigh Hunt
Samuel Laurence, c.1837
This portrait captures Hunt's boyish resilience and sense of mischief, even at the age of fifty-three. 'He was rather tall,' wrote his son Thornton admiringly, 'as straight as an arrow, and looked slenderer than he really was … His eyes were black and shining, his general complexion dark' (Preface to *Autobiography*).

Hunt's 'feckless' personality was later caricatured as Skimpole in Dickens's *Bleak House*. His family had black Caribbean roots and all his life he felt an outsider in England, his sunny bohemian temperament and sprightly verse-writing – 'Abou Ben Adhem, may his tribe increase' (1834), 'Jenny kissed me' (1838) – bravely masking depressions, debts, much domestic unhappiness (chiefly involving his sister-in-law) and permanent discomfort in the cold English climate.

But he was a warm-hearted and generous man who loved pranks, parties and nicknames, and always referred to John Keats as 'Junkets'. Byron in turn referred to Leigh Hunt as 'Leontius', the lion-like freedom fighter, in humorous recognition of his independence as an editor.

John Keats (1795 –1821)

Though he became the epitome of the young, beautiful, doomed poet of late English Romanticism, Keats struck everyone who knew him with his tremendous energy, his robust good humour and his zest for living. The son of a stables manager from the East End of London, he was built rather like a flyweight boxer: short, stocky, with disproportionate broad shoulders and a strong, open face with a powerful, bony nose. Sensuous and highly intelligent, a lover of good claret and good company, he said poetry should be 'felt on the pulses'.

Apprenticed for four years to an apothecary, he applied in 1815 to study surgery at Guy's Hospital, where he walked the wards and attended medical lectures, while reading widely in seventeenth- and eighteenth-century English literature.

In 1816 he had the good fortune to meet Leigh Hunt, who published his sonnet 'On First Looking into Chapman's Homer' in *The Examiner*. Valuable friendships with Hazlitt, B.R. Haydon, Lamb, the young poet John Hamilton Reynolds and Shelley (not altogether easy) quickly followed and helped Keats's work to develop with astonishing speed and confidence. He published a first volume of *Poems* in 1817 and his first extended work, *Endymion*, in 1818. Though scathingly attacked in *Blackwood's Magazine*, as the adolescent member of the 'Cockney School', he went on undaunted with his verse-epic *Hyperion*. During these hectic and exciting years he wrote a series of superb letters on poetry, many to his brothers George and Tom and his sister Fanny, which contain his most influential ideas: imagination as 'Negative Capability' (partly drawn from Coleridge), art as 'disinterested', style as 'fine excess' and life as 'a vale of

John Keats
William Hilton after Joseph Severn, c.1822

Soul-making'. When Tom died of consumption, Keats moved
to his friend Charles Armitage Brown's house on the edge of
Hampstead Heath; their next-door neighbour was the eighteen-
year-old Fanny Brawne, with whom he fell passionately in love.

In the twelve months from September 1818, Keats produced
an outpouring of major poetry which is unmatched in English:
'The Eve of St Agnes', 'Ode to a Nightingale', 'Ode on
Melancholy', 'Ode to Psyche', 'Ode on a Grecian Urn', 'La Belle
Dame sanse Merci' (again partly inspired by Coleridge), 'Lamia'

and the quintessential poem of Keatsian ripeness, 'To Autumn'. They were all published in July 1820 and Keats's future seemed assured. But that spring he had begun spitting up arterial blood (which, as a medical student, he instantly recognised as the symptom of consumption), and in September he sailed for Italy with his friend Joseph Severn, hoping the southern climate might bring a remission from the fatal illness. Keats wrote no more poetry and died in a tiny apartment above the Spanish Steps in Rome in February 1821. Listening to the plashing Bernini fountain in the piazza below his window, he framed his own epitaph: 'Here lies one whose name was writ in water.' His poetry has flowed out to generations of readers ever since.

Keats was often sketched by his friends Severn, Brown and Haydon (who also made a life mask), and was perceptively observed by Hunt:

John Keats
Charles Armitage Brown, 1819

His shoulders were very broad for his size; he had a face in which energy and sensibility were remarkably mixed up, and eager power checked and made patient by ill-health. Every feature was at once strongly cut and delicately alive. If there was any faulty expression it was in the mouth which was not without something of a character of pugnacity. The face was rather long than otherwise ... the chin was bold, the cheeks sunken; the eyes mellow and glowing, large dark and sensitive. (*Lord Byron and Some of His Contemporaries*, 1828)

William Hilton's famous picture of Keats brooding over his manuscript book of poems, and perhaps foreseeing his own death, turns out to be posthumous. It is a careful amalgamation of several visual sources: Severn's ivory miniature (1819), Hilton's own chalk drawing, also done from life (1820), and the death mask made in Rome (1821). It was actually painted as a souvenir for Keats's friend Richard Woodhouse, probably in 1822 (see page 111).

Joseph Severn also went to enormous pains to reconstruct a remembered image of Keats in the study at Wentworth Place, Hampstead, when he had just completed the 'Ode to a Nightingale' in spring 1819. Severn actually began it in Rome in autumn 1821, several months after Keats's death, and over two years added meticulous authenticating details: 'the room, the open window, the carpet and chairs are all exact portraits, even to the mezzotint portrait of Shakespeare given him by his old landlady in the Isle of Wight' (*Letters*, 1859). In these works, Romantic portraiture has taken on a new emotional impulse, a conscious tribute to lost genius, a secular form of sacred iconography. They appear to be vividly realistic 'likenesses', but they are really pious memorials.

John Clare (1793–1864)

The last in a long line of eighteenth-century 'ploughboy' poets, Clare arrived in London from Northamptonshire in 1820 with the straw still clinging to his worsted jacket. He was the son of a farm labourer from the village of Helpstone, near Peterborough, and had taught himself to write poetry while working as a hedge-setter and lime-burner. Influenced by Crabbe and Goldsmith rather than Wordsworth, he brought a late flowering of the Romantic sensibility to a realistic knowledge of agricultural work and farming landscapes.

Clare's first book, *Poems Descriptive of Rural Life and Scenery* (1820), was published by Keats's bookseller, Taylor and Hessey

John Clare
William Hilton, 1820
Hilton's moving portrait, which captures Clare's extraordinary mixture of innocence and painful anxiety, was commissioned by his publisher, Taylor, in the first flush of his perilous London celebrity of 1820.

of Fleet Street, with an advance of £100. It sold out within two months and Clare became the darling of the London literary season, meeting Hazlitt, Hunt, Lamb and Coleridge. It was followed by *The Village Minstrel* (1821), *The Shepherd's Calendar* (1827) and *The Rural Muse* (1835). Clare's poetry, with exquisite and earthy observations of the natural world (dung as well as dew-drops), is suffused by a sense of loss and an awareness of hardships and the unfeeling cruelty of the great landlords. His life became increasingly disturbed and unhappy as the vogue for his poetry declined, and in 1837 he was admitted to an insane asylum at Epping. Though married to a faithful wife, Martha Turner, he came to believe he was living with his first, abandoned love, Mary Joyce. After escaping to rejoin Mary in 1841, he spent the rest of his life in Northampton General Asylum, continuing to pour out poetry that remained largely unpublished for many years. The full text of his Romantic satire, *The Parish*, was only published from a manuscript in Peterborough Museum in 1985.

When Clare first came to London at the age of twenty-seven, he was a thin, wiry figure with long sideburns and a fine country bloom upon his cheeks. But his deep-set eyes and prominent cheekbones already told of suffering and inner turmoils. The society writers gushed over his acute, natural sensitivity: 'What life in the eyes! What ardent thirst for excellence, and what flexibility and susceptibility to outward impression in the quivering lips!' (T.G. Wainewright, *The London Magazine*, 1821).

The editor Thomas Hood met him at a smart dinner party, nervously sipping a tankard of ale and shining 'verdantly' amidst the urban literati: 'in his bright grass-coloured coat and yellow waistcoat (there are greenish stalks, too, under the table) he looks a very cowslip' (*The London Magazine*, 1823).

Jane Austen (1775–1817)

It still seems paradoxical that the outstanding English novelist of the turbulent Romantic age should be the decorous, unmarried daughter of a Hampshire clergyman. Jane Austen cheerfully announced that 'three or four families in a Country Village is the very thing to work on' (Letters, 1814), and modestly declared that her books were ladylike miniatures, 'the little bit (two Inches wide) of Ivory on which I work with so fine a brush, as produces little effect after much labour' (Letters, 1816). Yet her subtle, often scathing comedies of courtship and cross-purposes have a universal human resonance. She was passionately dedicated to her art, wrote and rewrote relentlessly, and called

Jane Austen
Unknown artist, c.1810–15

Jane Austen
Cassandra Austen, c.1810

her novels her 'darlings'. Growing up at the bustling Steventon rectory (two of her brothers became admirals), she had produced a romantic novella *Love and Friendship* by the age of fourteen (her two heroines 'fainted alternately on a sofa'); and an illustrated *History of England* at fifteen ('by a partial, prejudiced and ignorant Historian'). Early drafts of her first three novels – which eventually became *Sense and Sensibility* (1811), *Pride and Prejudice* (1813), and *Northanger Abbey* (1818) – were already completed before the age of twenty-five. She accepted a proposal of marriage one evening in December 1802, but after overnight consultation with her sister Cassandra, changed her mind the following morning. Cassandra remained Jane's closest confidante and produced the famous watercolour sketch (*c.*1810), though her niece Anna said the round, pert, sarcastic face was 'hideously unlike' her aunt. Cassandra called Jane 'the sun of my life, the soother of every sorrow' (*Letters*, 1817), and subsequently destroyed much of their correspondence. After a long, distracting interlude at Bath, they returned with their elderly mother to Hampshire (Chawton Cottage), where Austen rapidly completed her six major novels – now including *Mansfield Park* (1814), *Emma* (1816) and *Persuasion* (1818) – in an extraordinary burst of creative energy before her death, at the age of forty-two, from Addison's disease. The great historical novelist Walter Scott wrote: 'That young lady had a talent for describing the involvements and feelings and characters of ordinary life, which is the most wonderful I ever met with. The big Bow-Wow strain I can do myself like any now going, but [her] exquisite touch ... is denied me' (*Journal*, 1826).

Felicia Hemans (1793–1835)

Felicia Dorothea Browne is now remembered as 'Mrs Hemans', famous for her patriotic recitation piece 'Casabianca' (1826), based on an incident during the Battle of the Nile: 'The boy stood on the burning deck/ Whence all but he had fled …'. She was the most successful 'parlour poet' of her age, the darling of the new illustrated women's annuals such as *The Keepsake*, and from the 1820's outsold every other poet including Byron and Scott. She caught the stirring, recessional mood of late Romanticism in a number of hymn-like lyrics, celebrating death, domesticity and imperial duty: 'The Homes of England', 'The Graves of a Household' and 'The Palm Tree'. Her own domestic life was chaotic: abandoned by her father, who emigrated to Quebec, and later by her husband, who absconded to Italy, Felicia gallantly supported herself and her five sons with a prodigious outpouring of more than twenty books of travel, poetry and plays. Her outstanding work, *Records of Women* (1828) is a landmark collection of exclusively female voices. Its startling, bitter dramatic poems and monologues include 'The Indian Woman's Death Song', 'Arabella Stuart', 'Joan of Arc', 'The American Forest Girl' and 'Properzia Rossi' (a forgotten Renaissance sculptress).

Tall, beautiful and alarmingly business-like, Felicia befriended a number of struggling women writers such as Mary Tighe, Laetitia Landon and Joanna Baillie. On her early

OPPOSITE
Mrs Felicia Hemans
Edward Smith after Edward Robertson, published 1837

Felicia Hemans
Angus Fletcher, 1829
'Imagine my dismay on visiting
Mr Fletcher's sculpture-room,'
she wrote ironically to a friend,
'on beholding at least six Mrs
Hemans, placed as if to greet
me in every direction. There
is something frightful in this
multiplication of oneself to
infinity' (Letter, July 1830).

death at the age of forty-two, Wordsworth put her into his
literary pantheon, his 'Extemporary Elegy' (1836), the only
woman poet alongside Coleridge, Lamb, Crabbe and Scott.
But her later popularity among Victorians, and some clever
parodies by Noël Coward ('The Stately Homes of England'),
reduced her reputation to a few well-worn classroom favourites
(often assumed to be written by Kipling) until she was recently
rediscovered by modern feminists.

J.M.W. Turner (1775–1851)

Landscape, seascape and history painter of revolutionary force, Turner gloriously reinvented the appearances of light, wind and water. He memorably embodied the mysterious, energised universe of the Romantic poets, and triumphantly anticipated French Impressionism. His contemporary, John Constable described his work as 'airey visions, painted with tinted steam'. Much of it was done on a series of annual sketching tours, at first to 'picturesque' regions of Britain (Wales, the Lake District, the Highlands) and later abroad to France, the Swiss lakes, Italy and Germany. He kept extensive

J.M.W. Turner
George Dance, 1800

travel journals, filled over three hundred sketchbooks and scribbled a mass of poetry to caption his pictures.

Turner exhibited his first painting at the Royal Academy at the age of fifteen, was appointed Associate RA at twenty-four, and elected Professor of Perspective at thirty-two (1807). He achieved early popular success with atmospheric Wordsworthian scenes like *Buttermere Lake* (1798), dramatic views of Nelson's sea battles like *Trafalgar as seen from the Mizzen Shroud of the Victory* (1806), and his epic 'narrative landscapes' including *Snow Storm: Hannibal and his Army Crossing the Alps* (1812), reflecting Napoleon's doomed ambitions. In the 1830s he became the favoured artist to illustrate the *Collected Poetical Works* of Byron, Scott, Rogers and Campbell. In John Doyle's imaginary conversation piece *Samuel Rogers at his Breakfast Table in 1815* (1823), Turner's small alert figure appears standing behind Byron (see page 12).

He always kept several secret studios in London (including a houseboat on the Thames), and cultivated a certain gruff misanthropy which, like his incongruous stovepipe hats, was designed to protect. He was generous to his students, slept with a series of pretty housekeepers, and probably fathered at least two children (Evalina and Georgiana), to whom he was greatly attached. He never stopped pushing the boundaries of vision, and produced his late Romantic masterpiece *Rain, Steam and Speed: The Great Western Railway* in 1844. His work puzzled and impressed Hazlitt: 'they are pictures of the elements ... the artist delights to go back to the first chaos of the world ... pictures of nothing, and very like' (*On Imitation*, 1817). Later he was championed by Ruskin in *Modern Painters* (1843). He died at his studios in Chelsea, where he was living incognito with his latest landlady, Sophia Booth, and known familiarly by riverside locals as 'good old Admiral Booth'.

J.M.W. Turner
John Linnell, 1838

The Forgotten Romantics

It is safe to say that not one person in a thousand will have heard of the beautiful Mary Blachford (1772–1810), read a line of her poetry or previously seen her entrancing picture (which is actually a miniature on ivory, no bigger than a beer mat). At seventeen she fell in love with the Anglo-Irish MP Henry Tighe, but their subsequent marriage was unhappy and childless, her one novel was never completed and she died from consumption at the age of thirty-eight (but see Bibliography).

Yet in 1811 a major Romantic poem in six cantos, *Psyche, or The Legend of Love*, was published posthumously 'by the late Mrs Henry Tighe' and went through five English and American editions. She was praised by Thomas Moore, eagerly discussed

....
LEFT
Mary Tighe
attributed to John Comerford
after George Romney, 1794–5

....
OPPOSITE
Mary Tighe Memorial
John Flaxman, 1815

by Shelley and admired by Keats when he was writing *Endymion* in 1817, though he later felt he had grown out of her: 'Mrs Tighe and James Beattie once delighted me – now I see through them and can find nothing in them ... yet how many they will still delight!' (*Letters*, 1819). The Tighe family erected a flamboyant tomb to her memory in Ireland, designed by John Flaxman (1815), in which the figure of a winged Psyche archly meditates upon her poetic slumbers. Felicia Hemans made a special pilgrimage there, and published an immensely popular and lachrymose poem in her honour, 'The Grave of a Poetess', in 1827.

The irony of Mary Tighe's subsequent slide into literary oblivion suggests what has become the most notable absence from the Romantic circle as we now look back on it. So many of the gifted women writers of the period, once praised and celebrated by their contemporaries, are now virtually unknown to modern readers. They have also become cruelly invisible, as even the archives of the National Portrait Gallery retain scant visual records, because so few portraits were commissioned or bequeathed by their friends, family, lovers, husbands or publishers.

Elizabeth Inchbald
George Dance, 1794

Laetitia Elizabeth Landon
Daniel Maclise, c.1830–5

Ann Yearsley
Henry R. Cook, 1814

There is one drawing of the Jacobin novelist and playwright Elizabeth Inchbald (1753–1821), who was spurned in love by William Godwin; one engraving of the poet and novelist Laetitia Landon (1802–38) who committed suicide at a remote slave-trade outpost in West Africa; one mezzotint of the self-educated poet Ann Yearsley (1756–1806), who supported herself with a daily milk-round in Bristol; one stipple engraving of the poet Charlotte Smith (1749–1806) of whom Wordsworth calmly wrote: 'A Lady to whom English verse is under greater obligations than are likely to be either acknowledged or remembered' (*Letters*, 1835).

There is no known portrait at all of the working-class poet from Kendal in the Lake District, Isabella Lickbarrow (even her dates are uncertain). She was the orphan of a Quaker schoolmaster, and roamed the hills of Cumberland, as she wrote in her *Poetical Effusions* of 1814:

> I, like the wild flowers of the mountains,
> That unknown unheeded lie,
> Like them shall leave a name unhonour'd
> And like them forgotten lie.

SELECT BIBLIOGRAPHY

1. Contemporary Sources

Samuel Taylor Coleridge, Notebooks: A Selection, ed. Seamus Perry (Oxford University Press, Oxford, 2002)

Thomas De Quincey, Recollections of the Lakes and the Lake Poets, 1839, ed. David Wright (Penguin, Harmondsworth, 1970)

Joseph Farington, Diaries, ed. Kenneth Garlick, 17 vols (Yale University Press, New Haven, 1998)

William Gilpin, Three Essays: On Picturesque Beauty; On Picturesque Travel; On Sketching Landscape (London, 1792)

Benjamin Robert Haydon, Autobiography and Journals (London, 1853)

William Hazlitt, The Spirit of the Age (London, 1825)

—— Conversations of James Northcote (London, 1827)

—— Essays on the Fine Arts (London, 1873)

Richard Payne Knight, An Analytical Enquiry Into the Principles of Taste (London, 1805)

John Opie, with a Memoir by Amelia Opie, Lectures on Painting (London, 1809)

Sir Joshua Reynolds, Discourses on Art, 1790, ed. R.R. Wark (Yale University Press, New Haven and London, 1975)

J.G. Lockhart, The Life of Robert Burns (Edinburgh, 1828) Memoirs of the life of Sir Walter Scott, 7 vols (Galignani, Paris, 1838)

Leigh Hunt, Autobiography (Smith, Elder and Co, London, 1850)

Henry Crabb Robinson, On Books and their Writers, ed. Edith Morley, 3 vols (J.H. Dent and Sons Ltd, London, 1938)

Mary 'Perdita' Robinson: Memoirs of the Late Mrs Robinson, Written by herself, edited by her daughter Mary Elizabeth Robinson, 4 vols (London, 1801)

William Godwin: Memoirs of the Author of A Vindication of The Rights of Woman, 1798, ed. Richard Holmes, (Penguin Classics, London, 1987)

Joseph Severn: Letters and Memoirs, edited by Grant F. Scott (Ashgate Books, Aldershot, 2005)

Edward John Trelawny, Records of Shelley, Byron and the Author (1858, revised 1878)

Dorothy Wordsworth, Journals 1798–1803, ed. Mary Moorman (Oxford University Press, Oxford, 1978)

2. Select Modern Biographies (alphabetically by subject)

Jane Austen: A Life, Claire Tomalin (Penguin Books, London, 1998)

Blake, Peter Ackroyd (Minerva, London, 1996)

Robert Burns: A Life, Ian McIntyre (Penguin Books, London, 2001)

Byron: Life and Legend, Fiona MacCarthy (Faber & Faber, London, 2002)

Coleridge: A Critical Biography, Rosemary Ashton (Blackwell, Oxford, 1996)

Coleridge: Early Visions and Coleridge: Darker Reflections, Richard Holmes, 2 vols (Harper Perennial, London, 2005)

John Clare, Jonathan Bate (Picador, London, 2003)

George Crabbe: An English Life 1754–1832, Neil Powell (Pimlico, London, 2004)

Humphry Davy: Science and Power, David Knight (Blackwell, Oxford, 1992)

Thomas De Quincey: The Opium Eater, Grevel Lindop (Dent, London, 1981)

The Godwins and the Shelleys, William St Clair (Faber & Faber, London, 1989)

The Day-Star of Liberty: William Hazlitt's Radical Style, Tom Paulin (Faber & Faber, London, 1998)

Hazlitt in Love, Jon Cook (Short Books, London, 2006)

Felicia Hemans: Selected Poems, Letters, Reception Materials, Susan J.Wolfson (Princeton University Press, New Jersey and Oxford University Press, Oxford, 2000)

The Herschel Chronicle, Constance Lubbock (Cambridge University Press, Cambridge, 1933)

Fiery Heart: The First Life of Leigh Hunt, Nicholas Roe (Pimlico, London, 2005)

Mrs Jordan's Profession, Claire Tomalin (Viking, London, 1994)

Edmund Kean: Fire from Heaven, Raymund Fitzsimons (Hamish Hamilton, London, 1976)

John Keats, Andrew Motion (Faber & Faber, London, 1997)

John Keats, Robert Gittings (Penguin Books, London, 2001)

Perdita: The Life of Mary Robinson, Paula Byrne (HarperCollins, London, 2004)

Perdita: Royal Mistress, Writer, Romantic, Sarah Gristwood (Bantam Press, London, 2005)

Robert Southey, Mark Storey (Oxford University Press, Oxford, 1997)

Mary Shelley, Miranda Seymour (John Murray, London, 2000)

Shelley: The Pursuit, Richard Holmes (Harper Perennial, London, 2005)

Mary Tighe, Miranda O'Connell (Somerville Press, Ireland, 2013)

Turner: A Life, James Hamilton (Hodder & Stoughton, London, 1997)

The Life and Death of Mary Wollstonecraft, Claire Tomalin (Penguin Books, London, 1992)

Mary Wollstonecraft: A Revolutionary Life, Janet Todd (Weidenfeld & Nicholson, London, 2000)

Mary Wollstonecraft: A New Genus, Lyndall Gordon (Little Brown, London, 2005)

William Wordsworth: A Life, Stephen Gill (Oxford Paperbacks, Oxford 1990)

William Wordsworth, Hunter Davies (Sutton Publishing, Stroud, 1997)

3. Specialist Studies

Frances Blanshard, Portraits of Wordsworth (George Allen & Unwin, London, 1959)

Anthony Burton and John Murdoch, Byron, exhibition catalogue (Victoria and Albert Museum, London, 1974)

Richard Godfrey, James Gillray: The Art of Caricature, exhibition catalogue (Tate Publishing, London, 2001)

Richard Holmes and David Crane, Romantics and Revolutionaries, exhibition catalogue (National Portrait Gallery, London, 2002)

Geoffrey Keynes, The Complete Portraiture of William and Catherine Blake (Trianon Press for William Blake Trust, London, 1977)

Iain McCalman (ed), An Oxford Companion to the Romantic Age: British Culture 1776–1832 (Oxford University Press, Oxford, 1999)

Richard Ormond, Early Victorian Portraits, 2 vols (The Stationary Office Books, London, 1973)

Morton D. Paley, Portraits of Coleridge (Oxford University Press, Oxford, 1999)

Donald Parson, Portraits of Keats (Cleveland World Pub. Co, New York, 1954)

David Piper, The Image of the Poet: British Poets and their Portraits (Clarendon Press, Oxford, 1982)

Desmond Shawe-Taylor, Genial Company: the Theme of Genius in Eighteenth-Century British Portraiture, exhibition catalogue (Nottingham University Art Gallery, Nottingham, and Scottish National Portrait Gallery, Edinburgh, 1987)

Jacob Simon, The Art of the Picture Frame (National Portrait Gallery, London, 1996)

William St Clair, The Reading Nation in the Romantic Period (Cambridge University Press, Cambridge, 2004)

Richard Walker, Regency Portraits, 2 vols (National Portrait Gallery, London, 1985)

Richard Wendorf, The Elements of Life: Biography and Portraiture in Stuart and Georgian England (Clarendon Press, Oxford, 1990)

Richard Wendorf, Sir Joshua Reynolds: the Painter in Society (National Portrait Gallery, London, 1996)

Carol Wilson and Joel Hafner (eds), Re-visioning Romanticism: British Women Writers 1776–1837 (University of Pennsylvania Press, Philadelphia, 1994)

Robert Woof and Stephen Hebron, Romantic Icons, exhibition catalogue (The Wordsworth Trust, Dove Cottage, Grasmere, 1999)

Jonathan Wordsworth and Stephen Hebron, Romantic Women Writers, exhibition catalogue (The Wordsworth Trust, Dove Cottage, Grasmere, 1994)

Jonathan and Jessica Wordsworth (eds), The New Penguin Book of Romantic Poetry (Penguin Books, London, 2001)

LIST OF ILLUSTRATIONS

INDEX